S0-BSD-557

Rediscovering Jesus

Rediscovering Jesus

BY JACK FINEGAN

ASSOCIATION PRESS · NEW YORK

83

Preface

THE CHAPTERS in this book may be described as sermonic essays based on the life of Jesus. All the subjects have been presented in public addresses. In their writing out as well as in their original delivery, the messages have had in view the interests and concerns of the ordinary reader and listener, although they have also been formulated in the light of scholarly research. Particularly it is hoped that in their present form they may speak to young people, college students and others of like age and thought. Above all, to whomever they come it is desired that they may bring something of the authentic call of Jesus Christ. In telling about a Sunday at Lambaréné, Albert Schweitzer once said: "Whatever I make my starting-point I always lead on to the innermost fact involved in becoming a Christian, namely, the being led captive by Christ, so that even the man who is only present at one service can get an inkling of what it really is to be a Christian."[1] I would like to do the same.

JACK FINEGAN

[1] Notes will be found at the end of the book.

Contents

vii

Rediscovering Jesus

Introduction

In the Fulness of Time

IT WAS characteristic of the apostle Paul to think in large terms. When he spoke of his work he outlined a grand strategy. "From Jerusalem and as far round as Illyricum," he wrote to the Romans, "I have fully preached the gospel of Christ."[1] These were the boundaries of the East. He had proclaimed the message in the strategic centers between them; now he was ready to turn to the West. When he thought of mankind he summed up all humanity in two men, the one, Adam, in whom all die, the other, Christ, in whom all shall be made alive.[2] When he considered the coming of Jesus Christ, he saw his appearance as taking place at the crucial and climactic moment in history. "But when the fulness of the time came," he wrote, "God sent forth his Son."[3]

The Greek word for time which Paul uses here is *chronos,* from which we derive "chronology." It refers to time in the sense of duration. In the long ongoing of history a completeness of circumstances was achieved which provided the appropriate moment for the life of Christ. Elsewhere Paul employs the other Greek word for time, *kairos,* which means a fixed and definite period, or a seasonable and opportune time. Thus he affirms that the work of Christ was done in "due season" or at the "right time."[4] *"Kairos,"* says Paul Tillich, "is fulfilled time, the moment of time which is invaded by eternity."[5] According to Paul the apostle, a special moment came and it was then that the invasion of time by eternity transpired which he recognized in Jesus Christ.

Historical study of the ancient world leads to the conclusion that there actually was a remarkable condition of readiness for something specially significant to happen at the very time when Jesus lived. In his book, *The Environment of Early Christianity,* S. Angus declares: "God makes no mistakes in history, Christianity came indeed 'in the fulness of the time,' and . . . the Graeco-Roman world was . . . in a wonderful state of preparation for the Kingdom."[6]

MATERIALLY READY

This state of preparation may be noticed first on the material side. Geographically, the known western world formed a unit. It was centered around the Mediterranean Sea, and a line drawn five hundred miles back from the shores of that sea would have enclosed its area. Outside that line were barbarian Huns on the north, fierce Parthians on the east, the wastes of the Sahara desert on the south, and the ocean and the supposed end of the world on the west. Inside that line was a natural, pleasant, and beautiful home of civilization, in approximately the same latitude as California and similar to it in many other ways including climate.

As far as transportation was concerned, facilities were enjoyed which were at least as adequate as those of any time prior to the modern steamship, railroad, automobile, and airplane. By wind and oars men were carried across the sea on many known and navigable routes; on horse and foot they proceeded along excellent roads and across well-built bridges. Flying over Transjordan today, the routes of such roads may still be traced, some disappearing now under the expanded waters of the Dead Sea. Fifteen feet beneath the Corso Umberto Primo, splendid thoroughfare of present-day Rome, are found the lava paving blocks of the ancient Via Lata. In the Roman Forum stood at that time the Miliarium Aureum, a golden milepost erected by Augustus. On it could be read the names and distances of the chief cities to which roads led, from Jerusalem on the east to London on the west. Due to such advantages, Julius Caesar could send a letter from one end of Europe to the other as fast as Napoleon could; and Paul could travel as swiftly as John Wesley.

Commerce naturally took advantage of these multiplied facilities of intercourse, to weave a widespread web of trade. Grain ships plied the Mediterranean; caravans moved along the highways. Jewish, Syrian, Greek, and Roman merchants settled abroad. Rome became a great emporium into which came an abundant "cargo of gold, silver, jewels and pearls, fine linen, purple, silk and scarlet, all kinds of scented wood, all articles of ivory, all articles of costly wood, bronze, iron and marble, cinnamon, spice, incense, myrrh, frankincense, wine, oil, fine flour and wheat, cattle and sheep, horses and chariots, and slaves."[7]

Linguistically, the confusion of Babel was as nearly overcome as it has ever been. Hebrew, Aramaic, classical Greek, and Latin still prevailed in their respective fields, but almost everywhere a common form of the Greek language was spoken and understood. Although doubtless lacking the perfectly balanced clauses of Demosthenes' rhetorical periods, and the fine discriminations of the other classical writers, this language of the everyday was almost ideally suited to the purpose for which it was used, the communication of the thoughts of all the people. Known to us from thousands of papyrus letters and documents recovered from the sands of Egypt, it speaks in a way readily translatable into the vernacular of our own time.

Jews, Greeks, and Romans made up the three branches of the human family living within this world. Diverse in character, their endowments were really complementary. Of the Jews, one of their own number said, "He hath set eternity in their heart,"[8] and a passionate, even fanatical devotion to their religion and their God distinguished them. The Greeks began with man rather than with God. Independent and original in thought, they deemed it good that man should know himself and enjoy all things, but in moderation. The genius of the Romans was in organization. Assimilating what others offered, they built massive works of architecture, an enduring code of laws, and a long-lived empire.

The government of the world by the Romans brought it the longest continuous period of comparative freedom from war ever known before or since. Erecting a rampart against the barbarians without, consolidating a variety of provinces within, and bringing both sea and land under the sway of law and order, they in-augurated a period of peace, the benefits of which were most gratefully received by peoples utterly weary of the internecine strife of the Greek states and the civil wars of Alexander's successors.

Thus it was that a number of factors worked together to produce an unusual state of interrelatedness among men and of quiet at the very time that Jesus lived. This situation was summarized by Origen, writing in the third century A.D., in these words: "In the days of Jesus, righteousness arose and fulness of peace; it began with his birth. God prepared the nations for his teaching, by caus-ing the Roman emperor to rule over all the world; there was no longer to be a plurality of kingdoms, else would the nations have been strangers to one another, and so the apostles would have found it harder to carry out the task laid on them by Jesus, when he said, 'Go and teach all nations.' "[9]

SOCIALLY NEEDY

At the same time that external circumstances were so arranged as to provide a unique opportunity for the reception and spread of a new idea in the world, the internal life of society witnessed to the existence of certain profound needs. It is clear from all that has been described thus far that there ought to have been one world, but there was not. Instead of a truly unified and harmonious society to which so many factors were obviously pointing, there were great and unbridged chasms within the common life.

From the point of view of the present it is possible to recognize that the Jews, Greeks, and Romans possessed complementary characteristics, the synthesis of which would have been of value to all. At the time, however, Jews and Gentiles were ranged against each other in irreconcilable antagonism. The stubborn separatism of the Jews, which was emphasized increasingly from the time of Ezra on, was answered by the anti-Semitism of which the gratuitous provocations engineered by Pontius Pilate and the other Roman procurators in Judea were an expression. The end result was the costly and devastating Great War of the Jews and Romans, the climactic point of which was the destruction of Jerusalem in A.D. 70.

Slaves and masters represented the two sides of another fundamental antagonism of the time. Both were men, but the ones were treated as things, and the others were corrupted by the absoluteness of their own power. When the book of Revelation catalogues the commercial cargoes of the time, it mentions slaves along with cattle and sheep, horses and chariots, but adds concerning the slaves, "that is, human souls."[10] Usually, however, this inalienable dignity of even the lowliest man was not remembered, and slaves were bought and sold like any other objects of merchandise, were subjected to frightful punishments if they ran away or rebelled, and were sent to death at the whim or for the amusement of their lords. In a single day at the Delos market, ten thousand slaves were sold. Even the great Augustus records, in the narrative of his public life and works inscribed on the monument at Ancyra, how he delivered thirty thousand slaves to their masters for execution. Trajan sent ten thousand slaves to mutual slaughter to amuse the populace of Rome.

Even men and women were in a sense arrayed against each other in that world. Despite notable exceptions, women generally occupied a low position, and men assumed an authority of ownership or lordship.

Such were some of the cleavages in the social order, and it was to precisely these that Paul alluded when he made his plea for a more inclusive order in Christ: "There is neither Jew nor Greek, there is neither slave nor free, there is neither male nor female; for you are all one in Christ Jesus."[11]

Furthermore, the people of that time ought to have been happy but were not. On the whole they were pessimistic about history. They believed that history was decline, a degenerative succession of ages of gold, silver, bronze, and iron. Or they thought that history was revolution in circles, a ceaseless cycle from which there was no escape.

They were fatalistic about life. Fate or Destiny appeared more powerful than the gods themselves. Stoicism, the chief ethical force of the time, was a system of fatalism in which there was no expectation of help from God or sympathy from man.

Many were frantic in the pursuit of pleasure. More and more exciting entertainment had to be devised to stimulate the jaded sensibilities of the blasé. The athletic contests of the Greeks gave way to the chariot races and gladiatorial shows of the Romans. Both the rich and the poor made idleness their favorite occupation. Juvenal's epigram summarized the situation in his day: "The public has long since cast off its cares; the people now longs eagerly for just two things—Bread and Circuses!"

To a considerable extent, men were debased in morality. Abandonment and killing of children, divorce and unnatural relations, were common. Not only Paul in his letters but also the Stoics in their street preaching drew up catalogues of vices, the documentation of which was only too evident on every hand.

People were tired of living. Idleness brought weariness, and self-indulgence brought satiety. Menander observed that "life and pain are akin." Livy said, "We can neither cure nor endure our vices." And Seneca noted, "Men complain that the hours drag too slowly past."

They were also afraid of dying. This was covered with a show of bravado or cynicism, which hardly hides the fundamental nihilism and hopelessness of outlook. On many graves of the time appear the initials NFFNSNC. These stand for an affirmation so familiar then that it no longer had to be written out in full: *Non fui, fui, non sum, non curo,* "I was not, I was, I am not, I care not." Also frequently repeated is the advice: *Es, bibe, ludi, veni,* "Eat, drink, play, come hither." Other epitaphs read: "Horror does not seize me when I think of the putrefaction of my body; nothing further touches us"; "What I have eaten and drunk, that I take with me; what I have left behind I have forfeited"; "All is laughter, all is dust, all is nothing."

Once again, their religions ought to have saved them but did not. The old paganism was largely impotent. The educated laughed at the popular gods, who had been quite devoid of moral authority ever since Xenophanes remarked that "Homer and Hesiod ascribe to the gods everything that among men is a shame and disgrace." Judaism was increasingly encased in a shell of legalism. So numerous were the rules and regulations which it prescribed that many refrained from accepting any of them since they could not possibly keep all of them. The new religions, compounded of Oriental elements, exercised the fascination of the mysterious but proved to embody much superstition. Indeed superstition, miracle mongering, fortune telling, and fantastic salvation rituals found all too ready an acceptance in a world which, according to Gilbert Murray, had experienced a "failure of nerve."

SPIRITUALLY HOPEFUL

And yet, despite everything, there was a certain thrill of hope and expectancy running through the ancient world. The Gentiles were seeking for something better than they had. Recognition of the evils in society, on the one hand, and the development of a sense of the dignity of man and the brotherhood of men, on the other, combined to produce a more favorable moral climate. In religion there was a growing feeling that "the best can only be One," as Xenophanes had said, and a striving toward a universal faith—a not too successful example being the emperor worship in which it was sought to unify a far-flung empire. Individual persons practiced self-examination and sought self-improvement, as did Seneca, who every evening examined his deeds and words of the past day, declaring, "Why should I hesitate to face my shortcomings when I can say, 'Take care not to repeat them, and so I forgive you today'?" Many desired a personal savior and thought wistfully of personal immortality. "They were stretching out their hands in longing for the farther shore," said Virgil. They were asking the question which Seneca phrased: "Where shall He be found whom we have been seeking for so many centuries?"

The Jews were expecting the Messiah. Perhaps it was their influence which spread abroad and stimulated the hopes of others. Or perhaps their expectation was only a special example of a more universal yearning which could be attested all the way from the Zoroastrian belief in the future coming of Saoshyant, for the renovation of the universe, to the anticipation expressed by Virgil that a providentially sent deliverer would arise to cleanse mankind of guilt and raise it to a higher life. At any rate there was never a more beautiful statement of hope for a coming King than that which stands in the book of Isaiah:

> *The people that walked in darkness*
> *Have seen a great light;*
> *Those who dwelt in a land of deep darkness—*
> *On them has light shone. . . .*
> *For every boot worn by booted warrior in the fray,*
> *And war cloak stained with blood,*
> *Will be for burning—food for the fire.*
> *For a child is born to us, a son is given to us;*
> *And the government will be upon his shoulder;*
> *And his name will be called*
> *"Wonderful counselor is God almighty,*
> *Father forever, Prince of peace."*
> *Of the increase of his government, and of peace,*
> *There will be no end. . . .*
> *The zeal of the Lord of hosts will do this.*[12]

Such was the world into which Jesus was born, a world materially ready for a great event to happen, socially needy, and spiritually hopeful. It was strikingly like our own world. Now it is no longer the Mediterranean Sea but the frontierless ocean of the air itself which provides a medium for transportation, commerce, and communication. Now, too, three great peoples of complementary characteristics but presently conflicting purposes meet —the Caucasoid, the Mongoloid, and the Negroid. The inescapable proximity of each to the other and the undeniable consanguinity of all indicate that men belong to one human family, but the one world to which these considerations point eludes us still. Peace of mind for the individual often remains, like peace for the world, a wistful but unrealized hope. Even religion has yet to demonstrate its full power to meet the present crisis. But if the hope, long ago, that something wonderful would happen was abundantly justified by the actual life of Jesus Christ, it behooves us to study his life with the like hope that in him we too will find that which we most need.

Part 1: The Fact of Christ

CHAPTER TWO

The Historic Jesus[1]

A T THE time when Jesus lived, many circumstances combined to produce a situation specially favorable for the founding of a new religion, and many hopes were expressed for the coming of a deliverer. Is it possible that the situation itself created the religion which emerged, and that the very strength of men's hopes led them to imagine that a figure had appeared who fulfilled those hopes? Has it ever been doubted if Jesus really lived?

THE RISE OF DOUBT

Yes, men have questioned the historicity of Jesus. Since Descartes, it has been held that the pursuit of truth requires the critical scrutiny of every inherited tradition and belief, and the retention of only that which cannot possibly be doubted. "The first rule was," wrote the seventeenth century founder of modern philosophy, "never to receive anything as a truth which I did not clearly know to be such . . . and not to comprehend anything more in my judgments than that which should present itself so clearly and so distinctly to my mind that I should have no occasion to entertain a doubt of it."

By the eighteenth century this kind of doubt was directed toward the historical existence of Jesus. Voltaire said, "I have taken as my patron saint St. Thomas of Didymus, who always insisted on an examination with his own hands," and concluded a consideration of the life of Jesus with these words, "It is necessary whilst awaiting faith to limit oneself to drawing this conclusion: There did exist an obscure Jew from the dregs of the people named Jesus who was crucified as a blasphemer in the time of the Emperor Tiberius, it being impossible to determine in which year." Twenty years after the death of Voltaire, another Frenchman, Charles François Dupuis, stated his belief that it was possible to explain Jesus as an astral myth: "When we shall have shown that the pretended history of a God, resuscitated at Easter or at the Vernal equinox, after having descended into hell, who brings with Him a retinue of twelve apostles whose chief possesses all the attributes of Janus— a God, conqueror of the prince of darkness, who translates mankind into the empire of light, and who heals the woes of the world, is only a solar fable . . . it will be almost as unnecessary to inquire whether there was a man called Christ as it is to inquire whether some prince is called Hercules."

In the nineteenth century David Friedrich Strauss made a critical examination of the life of Jesus, and found in the New Testament records of that life a great deal of myth. The imagination of the writers, he held, influenced by the fairy stories of paganism and the miraculous narratives of the Old Testament, was responsible for much that was told. To Strauss that did not matter, however, for as a follower of Hegel he felt that all that was really important was the existence of the "idea of God-manhood," and of this idea the story of Jesus gave a symbolical account. Bruno Bauer went beyond Strauss to deny that Jesus ever lived. The movement of Christianity came into being, he explained, as an outcome of the conditions which prevailed in the ancient world. In Christianity, currents of thought mingled from Judea, Greece, and Rome. Its leading ideas came from Philo, Plato, Seneca, and others. The New Testament was not written until the second century, much of it after A.D. 150, and Jesus himself was purely a literary fiction.

In the twentieth century the most vehement denials of the historicity of Jesus were made. W. B. Smith in the United States, J. M. Robertson in England, G. J. Bolland in Holland, P. L. Couchoud in France, and Peter Jensen and Arthur Drews in Germany, all maintained that Jesus was only a myth. Smith thought that Christianity arose out of a Jesus-cult which already existed in the first century B.C. Robertson claimed that the figure of Jesus was a fictitious composite of ideas borrowed chiefly from the mystery religions. Bolland found that Jesus was none other than the Old Testament Joshua clothed in garments of Gnostic speculation. Couchoud said of Jesus: "Whatever he was at the beginning, whatever he has since become, the collective hopes of men made him. . . . The history of Jesus is not the elaboration of something which took place, but the expression of something which men passionately wished to take place: the suffering and death of a god that mankind might be saved."[2] Jensen declared that the story of Jesus, and that of Paul as well, were variants of the Gilgamesh epic of ancient Babylonia. "Of the career of the alleged founder of Christianity we know nothing," he said. "We serve in our cathedrals and houses of prayer, in our churches and schools, in palace and hut, a Babylonian god, Babylonian gods." Drews wrote voluminously about the "Christ myth" and concluded: "The fact is that there is *nothing, absolutely nothing,* either in the actions or words of Jesus, that has not a mythical character or cannot be traced to parallel passages in the Old Testament or the Talmud, and is therefore under suspicion of being derived from them. . . . If all the details of the gospel story are resolved in mythical mist, as they are resolved in the hands of historical criticism, then . . . we lose all right, not merely to say what Jesus was, but to make the bare assertion that there ever was such a person."[3]

The Christ-myth theory proved more attractive than ever to some persons in the political upheavals with which the twentieth century was soon convulsed. In 1938, while Hitler was still master of Germany and Alfred Rosenberg was "educator" of the National Socialist Party, H. G. Wood of England published a fine book entitled *Did Christ Really Live?* Reviewing that book, William Robinson, then principal of Overdale College, asked why it was necessary for it to be written. He answered by pointing out that Dr. Rosenberg had not failed to exploit the stupidities of the Christ-myth school in the interests of his mission and that many had been beguiled thereby. Then Principal Robinson said: "Jesus has become decidedly inconvenient to a large part of the political world of our day. As a myth he might be harmless enough, but as a

Man who is the Center of History and the key to human destiny, ruling in the lives of his followers, he is intolerable."

THE METHODS OF INQUIRY

The historicity of Jesus has been questioned. Has it been studied scientifically? Yes. A classic account of the modern study of the life of Jesus was written by Albert Schweitzer in *The Quest of the Historical Jesus;* and the story was carried further by Chester C. McCown in a volume entitled *The Search for the Real Jesus.* Schweitzer, who has been called "the greatest man in the world today," was in his thirties when he wrote the book just mentioned. Then at the University of Strasbourg, he brought home all the Lives of Jesus which were to be found in the University Library, a great institution which possessed in fact practically everything of significance written up to that time. In his room Schweitzer arranged all of these volumes in piles on the floor according to the chapters in which they were later to appear in his book. McCown remarks, "One would not forget the harassed Swabian housekeeper who tried to sweep between the piles."

As he evaluated the undertaking which these books represented, Schweitzer said: "The world has never seen before, and will never see again, a struggle for truth so full of pain and renunciation as that of which the Lives of Jesus of the last hundred years contain the cryptic record." He called the research that had been carried out by German scholars "a uniquely great expression of sincerity, one of the most significant events in the whole mental and spiritual life of humanity."[4]

By what methods is this tremendous wrestle of men's best minds with historic reality carried on? There is linguistic study. The ancient languages which Jesus spoke and in which the New Testament was written are learned, and the papyri and other documents of the ancient world are sifted to find the usage of the various words. Textual study is another method. The most ancient manuscripts are sought out in remote corners of the world, and all are compared with painstaking care. Literary study is a part of the work. The gospels are written in parallel columns and studied word for word in the Greek in comparison with each other. Form criticism is the name of another technique. It is recognized that the materials in the gospels circulated orally before they were written down, and it is attempted to discover their original forms. Criticism by social environment is also employed. Here the attempt is made to test the genuineness of the materials by their relevance to the life-situation out of which they are supposed to have come. All of these are parts of one great historical method by which the life of Jesus is studied scientifically.

Summarizing such manner of study, one of its greatest exponents, Hans Lietzmann, wrote: "Facts have their own importance and demand their rights from serious science; they fight their way through and, in the end, hold the field. . . . In spite of all the transformation effected by tradition, we see in every direction the genuine rock of reliable information upon which the historian can build—if only he will deal with the sources of primitive Christianity by the same methods as all other sources in this world. That means, however, that he must stand over against them as an expert and disinterested judge, not as an accuser who is distrustful on principle. There is only one historical method; if we hear of special methods for religion, history, legend, form-criticism, and the history of worship, we must remember that these are not new methods but new standpoints calculated to supplement each other and to refine the one historical method."[5]

THE FACTS

What are the facts discovered in historical investigation if we conduct it, not as accusers "distrustful in principle," but as seekers, endeavoring as honestly and fairly as possible to weigh the evidence? Three main arguments have been advanced by those who have attacked the historicity of Jesus. First, they have declared that the records of his life are late and unreliable. Are they?

The oldest source is the letters of Paul. They were being written around A.D. 50. They were "occasional" letters dealing with specific situations and problems and their references to the historical life of Jesus are only incidental. For that very reason they are the more valuable. From them we learn such facts as that Jesus was born a Jew, and had several brothers including one named James whom Paul himself knew quite well. Jesus worked among the Jews, and some of them were responsible for his death, but he died by the Roman method of crucifixion. Before his death he ate a Last Supper with his disciples and at it broke bread and gave them a cup to drink, signifying his own body broken and his blood poured out for them. After his crucifixion he was buried, and raised from the dead. His character included the traits of righteousness, obedience, gentleness, humility, and complete absence of self-seeking. Here we have almost an outline of the life and character of Jesus, and it is to be found completely within the letters of Paul.

Did Paul perhaps invent all of this? Did he, for example, take the familiar Jewish hope for a Messiah and create a picture to correspond with it? Actually the picture which he gives us of Christ is at almost every point in flat contradiction to the expectations which prevailed among the Jewish people. They had anticipated a Messiah who would reign in power; Paul tells about one who walked in humility. They had expected one who would unite all Israel; Paul tells of one whom Israel rejected. The Christ for whom men looked was to vindicate the law; the Christ who came perished under the curse of the law. This picture of Jesus given by Paul was not invented by him; it came out of history. C. H. Dodd has summed up the matter in this way: "The Pauline testimony, therefore, is all of a piece. He attests the character of Jesus, something of His life and death, and something of His teaching; and he assigns Him His place in history as a crucified Messiah. This testimony is of the utmost importance, since we know that Paul came into the Church (which he already knew before his conversion) within seven years (probably less) from the Crucifixion; that he was well acquainted with Peter, John, and James, the brother of Jesus; and that for all their differences of opinion, he never differed from them in his conception of the fundamental tradition."[6]

Alongside this first great source of knowledge about the historic Jesus, stand, as a second major source, the synoptic gospels. These are the gospels which bear the names of Matthew, Mark, and Luke, and they are often called "synoptic" because they take more or less the same or a common view of the life of Jesus. Although it does not now stand first in the New Testament, the earliest of these was the gospel according to Mark. The author whose name the work bears was probably the Mark who was a companion of both Paul and Peter, as mentioned in the book of Acts and the first epistle of Peter. This gospel must have been written not later than around A.D. 70, and it was used extensively in the composition of both Matthew and Luke. These two gospels were based not only upon Mark but also upon a second foundation which was evidently a collection of the sayings of Jesus. It is a plausible guess that the latter originated as a compilation in the Aramaic language by the apostle Matthew, inasmuch as the ancient Papias, who lived early in the second century A.D., has left us a statement that Matthew collected the oracles of the Lord in the Hebrew language. In addition, Luke must have had a special source for not a little material, including the wonderful series of parables of Jesus which is included in this gospel. Not only that, there may well have been stories still circulating separately and even orally at this time, some of which were incorporated in the gospels as finally composed.

In studying these gospels it must be recognized that they are some distance removed from the lifetime of Jesus, and that within that space of time the tradition of what Jesus did and said was employed and even altered in accordance with the needs of the developing church; nevertheless it must be insisted that that church only came into existence because something wonderful had taken place, and that the church always considered it to be its first duty to tell what had transpired. In actuality, as the gospels are studied, beneath later accretions the outlines of unquestionably historical happenings stand forth massively.

Beyond the synoptic gospels is the fourth gospel, that according to John, which was probably composed around A.D. 100. It is acknowledgedly a philosophical and theological work, written out of long meditation and mostly concerned with the inner, spiritual meaning of the life of Christ. Nevertheless it contains data which supplement the synoptics. In particular, on the question of the date of the death of Jesus it provides information not found in the synoptics, and very probably correct. Using the facts set forth in John and consulting Babylonian astronomical and calendrical tables, A. T. Olmstead arrived at the conclusion that the crucifixion of Jesus took place on the eve of Passover, Friday, April 7, A.D. 30. This date may very well be exact. Olmstead himself declares: "Few indeed are the dates in Greek and Roman history before Julius Caesar's reforms which can pretend to anything like the same precision."[7]

How sure are we that we still have accurate copies of the ancient sources of which we have been speaking? By discovery in the sands of Egypt we now have a fragment of John's gospel dating, according to the style of its handwriting, in the first half of the second century A.D., and a copy of an entire collection of the letters of Paul dating from the beginning of the third century. From Mount Sinai and the Vatican come two other manuscripts belonging to the middle of the fourth century; after that there are many more. These manuscripts are far closer to the originals than in the case of any other ancient Greek book.

A second objection by those who deny the historicity of Jesus is that the Jews, among whom he lived, say little about him. This is true, but there is a reason for it. The reason is that Christianity and Judaism soon came into a lamentable conflict, and the Jewish writers therefore did not want to refer to the founder of the rival faith. In later ages, moreover, the Talmud itself was sometimes attacked by church authorities or censored by the Jews themselves in order to avoid persecution; consequently the passages which did mention Jesus are often missing or mutilated. According to the recent researches of Rabbi Morris Goldstein, however, there are at least five authentic references to Jesus in the Talmudic literature of the Tannaitic period, that is, prior to the year 220 of the Christian era. Of these, the two which speak most directly about Jesus himself make these statements: "On the eve of Passover they hanged Yeshu." "Yeshu had five disciples—Mattai, Nakkai, Netzer, Buni, and Todah."[8] The first statement is in agreement with the gospel according to John as to the time of the death of Jesus. The second contains names of disciples at least reminiscent of names which appear in the gospels, Mattai for Matthew, Todah for Thaddeus.

A third objection is that the Roman writers of the time do not mention Jesus. The reason for this is also apparent. It lies in the fact that, from their point of view, Palestine was only a distant, unimportant part of the Empire. When, however, they do have occasion to mention Jesus, as Tacitus did in telling of Nero's persecution of the Christians, they have the facts exactly right; for Tacitus declared that Jesus was put to death in the reign of the emperor Tiberius by the procurator Pontius Pilate.

The real facts, then, are that the records of the life of Jesus are not late and unreliable, but early and surprisingly dependable, and the references which the ancient Jews and Romans make to him are just such as we would expect, knowing the historical circumstances of the rise of Christianity. We may safely join H. G. Wood in giving an affirmative answer to the question which is the title of his book, *Did Christ Really Live?* This author writes of Jesus: "The demands put into his lips are stern and inexorable. It would be easier to evade their challenge if we could dissociate them from the actualities of history. If Jesus were the figment of popular imagination, he would be more manageable and less baffling, less humiliating and more negligible. In this region, one may suspect, lie the deeper reasons why the Christ-myth hypothesis appears attractive and credible to not a few. . . . But there at long last is the strange man on a cross—no myth, no phantom, but a man like and unlike ourselves. Try as we may, we cannot get him out of history, and if we have any sense for reality, we cannot evade his challenge."[9]

Does it matter whether Jesus really lived? Some say that it does not. If one believes something and derives benefit from it, they declare, it is a good thing even if it is not true. If the idea of Christ exists, they maintain, it is not important whether any such person ever actually lived or not. But we are in a realistic age.

If Christianity is founded upon an idle dream, it would be better to say so and cease deluding ourselves. Our religion professes to be based upon what God has done in history. If we have nothing to tell but legend and myth, Christianity is weak. It is strong because it is founded upon historical reality.

CHAPTER THREE

The Prophetic Jesus

W HAT IS the place of Jesus in the history of the world? That he is an actual part of that history cannot be doubted. He really lived on this earth somewhat more than nineteen hundred years ago. But in what line of thought and endeavor did he stand? What was his background and what was his purpose?

It is clear of course that Jesus lived as a member of the Jewish people. His descent was from David according to the flesh, as the apostle Paul puts it. The Jewish people were an integral part of the ancient world, yet a unique part of it. Having intimate contacts from the first with Mesopotamia and Egypt, and later brought into touch with Greece and Rome, they shared a great deal in common with their neighbors. Yet they made an unparalleled contribution to the intellectual life of mankind. There were trends toward monotheism in the ancient Orient, as exemplified by the short-lived reformation of Akhnaton, but it was Israel that actually launched in the world a living faith in one righteous God. There were movements toward a community of all men, as in the primitive democracy of Mesopotamia or the philosophers' republic of Plato, but it was in Israel that the cause of a lowly peasant was championed against the privilege of a king, and that every man was seen to have the inherent dignity of one made in the image of God. It is such conceptions that place the Jewish people more directly in line with the world of today than any other people of antiquity. As William A. Irwin puts it in discussing Israel's distinctive achievement in *The Intellectual Adventure of Ancient Man,* "the boundary between the ancient world and the modern is to be traced, not in the Aegean or the middle Mediterranean, but in the pages of the Old Testament."[1] These were the people among whom and as one of whom Jesus lived; by that very token he stands on this side of the boundary line between the ancient and the modern.

Among the Jewish people and in their religion, however, were many different emphases and specific lines of thought. There were the legalism of the Torah and Halakah, the dogmatism of the Haggadah, the sacrificial system of the priests, the prophecies of the prophets, the visions of the apocalyptic writers, the aphoristic wisdom of the wise men, the personal piety of the Psalmists, the pessimistic philosophy of Ecclesiastes, the nomadism of the Rechabites, the withdrawn life of the Essenes, the fiery patriotism of the Zealots. In which of these lines of thought did Jesus stand? With what type of endeavor did he associate himself? According to Matthew 5:17, it was not his purpose to destroy what had gone before in the religious heritage of his people, but to fulfill it. What in particular did Jesus bring to fulfillment and sum up in himself and his work?

It is now generally recognized that the prophets played a very important part in the great achievements of Israel in monotheism and ethics. It is therefore a reasonable supposition that it was the central prophetic emphasis in Judaism which, more than any other, Jesus summed up in himself. He stood in the line of succession of the prophets, he was the heir of what they had done, he fulfilled what they had anticipated, he brought to summation what was intimated in their writings. John W. Bowman states the thesis in these words in his book, *The Intention of Jesus:* "Jesus' culture was Hebraic . . . and within the limits of the Hebraic culture he took his stand squarely, knowingly, and without reservation, with the prophetic strand of that culture."[2]

Among the four gospels, that according to Mark was of special interest in relation to the historicity of Jesus because it was the oldest. In consideration of the prophetic nature of the life and work of Jesus, the gospel according to Matthew is particularly significant. At numerous points in the life of Jesus, what is narrated is connected with intimations of Old Testament prophecy, and extended quotations from the Old Testament are made. While the discovery and citation of many of these passages may have been the work of the compiler of the gospel, the very fact that he undertook to do this shows how strongly it was felt among the early Christians that the life of Jesus stood in integral relation to the central heritage of Judaism. Indeed the entire New Testament is witness to the same fact, for, according to one computation, there are no less than 275 quotations in it from the Old Testament.

What are the facts which support the thought that Jesus is the prophetic Christ? At least seven may be cited. First, Jesus quoted extensively from the Old Testament and mostly from the prophets. Even allowing generously for the editorial work of the gospel compilers in supplying relevant Old Testament material, it can scarcely be doubted that Jesus himself made frequent references to and quotations from the Scriptures of his own people. In a book entitled *The Religion of Maturity,* John W. Bowman has listed all the passages which Jesus is said in the gospels to have quoted from the Old Testament. When such a list is studied it is seen that the greatest number of quotations are from the books of the prophets, specially Isaiah, and after that from books like Deuteronomy and Psalms in which there is much of the spirit of the prophets.

Second, men thought about Jesus as a prophet. It was a widely held opinion that he was "a prophet, like one of the prophets of old."[3] When he asked who men said that he was, an answer was, "One of the prophets."[4] When he entered Jerusalem, the crowds said, "This is the prophet Jesus from Nazareth of Galilee."[5]

Third, he spoke of himself as a prophet. When he was rejected at Nazareth, he said, "A prophet is not without honor, except in his own country."[6] When he anticipated his death at Jerusalem, he stated, "It cannot be that a prophet perish out of Jerusalem."[7]

In the fourth place, Jesus described his mission in terms of the expectations of the prophets. When he spoke for the first time at Nazareth, marking out his mission, he quoted from the sixty-first chapter of Isaiah.[8] Toyohiko Kagawa, himself a person of prophetic spirit in the modern world, observes that in this quotation mention of preaching to the poor indicates the intention to do a work of economic emancipation; of healing the broken-hearted, a work of psychological emancipation; of proclaiming release to captives, a work of physical emancipation of men; of setting at liberty the oppressed, a work of political emancipation. It was the great ethical principles of the prophets which Jesus is thus said to have stressed in that inaugural sermon at Nazareth.

In the fifth place, Jesus enacted sayings of the prophets. It can hardly be an accident that his manner of entrance into Jerusalem at the last coincided so exactly with the words of Zechariah: "Rejoice greatly, O daughter of Zion; shout, O daughter of Jerusalem: behold, thy king cometh unto thee; he is just, and having salvation; lowly, and riding upon an ass, even upon a colt the foal of an ass."[9] Popular expectation looked for a military Messiah; here was a passage which described a king of a different kind, humble and helpful to all. If the work of an editor is to be sought in the account, it will be found in the change introduced by Matthew. Instead of the colt mentioned by Mark and Luke as the mount of Jesus, Matthew tells of both an ass and a colt, and relates that "the disciples . . . laid their coats upon them, and Jesus seated himself upon them."[10] The reason Matthew makes the situation as awkward as this is that he is trying to describe a scene which would literally reproduce the statement in Zechariah. But what we actually have in Zechariah is simply an example of the familiar Hebrew literary device of parallelism, where the mount of the king is mentioned twice, first as an ass, and then, with a slight variation in phraseology, as a colt, the foal of an ass. The very fact that such a literary change as Matthew has made is clearly discernible and clearly explicable only increases our feeling that the underlying event was a real historical happening. Jesus presented himself to Jerusalem, at his last coming here, in a way that represented one of the profoundest but not one of the most popular insights of the Old Testament.

As a sixth point, it may be noted that Jesus explained the purpose of his death in terms of prophetic ideas. God had made a covenant with the people of Israel a long time before. Mention of such a covenant is prominent particularly in the prophetic books of Hosea, Deuteronomy, and Jeremiah. But the people failed to live up to their part of this covenant, and that brought disaster upon them. Jeremiah, however, declared that in the future God would make a new covenant with the house of Israel. At the Last Supper Jesus declared that the cup which he gave his disciples to drink was his blood of the covenant which was poured out for many. In death he would seal the new agreement, which had been prophetically anticipated, between God and man with his own lifeblood.

In the seventh place, he presented himself as the fulfillment of prophetic hope. According to the gospels Jesus was the Christ, the Son of God, the suffering Servant, the Son of man. The Messiah or Christ, as the title etymologically signifies, was the one anointed by God to establish his kingdom. Kings, priests, and prophets were set apart for their work by anointing among the Hebrews. When hopes turned to the ideal king of the future it was natural to speak of him as the Anointed. The royal ruler was also characterized by divine sonship. This would hardly have been meant in the mythological way that such an idea would have been held in Egypt or Mesopotamia, but rather as an indication of divine providence and purpose in his rule. In Psalm 2 we read about the anointed ruler and hear how the Lord said to him, "Thou art my son."[11]

The Servant of the Lord who must suffer to perform his mission appears in the latter part of the book of Isaiah. The original reference is probably to the people of Israel who, through suffering, will bring true religion to the world. The people are personified in a single figure, however, and we read of "a man of sorrows,"[12] who bears the griefs of others and is wounded for their transgressions. The phrase "son of man" occurs in the Psalms as a poetic parallel for "man," and in Ezekiel in the sense of "mortal man."[18] In Daniel the same phrase describes a figure, evidently also personifying Israel, who appears before the Ancient of Days to receive an everlasting kingdom.

It is possible, and is maintained by some, that the application of some or all of these titles to Jesus was the work of his followers, who studied the Scriptures to gain light on his work, his sufferings, and his victory which they expected in the future. It is also possible, however, that it was he himself who took these ideas from the Scriptures to explain his own work. Certainly all four titles were at home upon Jewish soil, and while "Son of God" fitted in with Hellenistic ways of thought and experienced a wide usage and enlarged meaning in the Hellenistic world, "Son of man" was quite unintelligible there and quickly dropped out of currency almost completely. The idea of the suffering Servant was not used much there either, and "Christ" was soon forgotten to have been a title and was employed as a part of a personal name, as may be seen in the writings of Paul who speaks interchangeably of Jesus Christ, or Christ Jesus. It seems difficult to maintain, therefore, that these titles were all inventions of later Christianity as applied to Jesus. Furthermore, if that were to be held the case, it would also have to be explained why precisely these ideas were selected out of the larger mass of prophetic materials in the Old Testament, not a few of which were quite at disharmony with these. Actually, only certain concepts were chosen, and they were ones which fitted well together or were sufficiently transformed in their usage to be made to fit together. It is not likely, therefore, that the gospel portrait of the Christ was produced by the discovery and application of extraneous categories to one who had stood aloof from such, but rather resulted from what C. H. Dodd calls "the impact of historical fact."[14]

If, then, Jesus accepted from his disciples the confession of faith, "You are the Christ"[15]; if he declared that no one knew the Father "except the Son and any one to whom the Son chooses to reveal him"[16]; if on the eve of his death he quoted the words about the Servant, "And he was reckoned with transgressors"[17]; and if beyond death he envisioned himself as the Son of man receiving the eternal kingdom on behalf of his people—then indeed he offered himself as fulfilling the hopes of the prophets. In the words of William Manson, "The Messianic language used by Jesus for the explication of his destiny came as the final stamp upon an extraordinary sense of engagement to bring his nation to God. . . . The Messianic ideas of Israel functioned as the historical reagent which brought out the final significance of the revelation concerning God with which Jesus believed himself to be charged. . . . The Messianic confession of Christianity remains anchored to the historical personality and character of Jesus. . . . It is not a case of the human personality of Jesus being swallowed up in a Messianic conception, but of all Messianic conceptions being absorbed into the sphere of his spirit."[18]

THE NATURE OF HISTORY

To Jesus, who stands in history as the prophetic Christ, we may come with our questions about history. What is the nature of history? The Christian answer to this question has a distinctiveness which can only be appreciated in contrast with other ideas which have prevailed in the world. The people of the Orient have largely held that history is illusion. In the language of Indian philosophy, history is Maya, a veil of unreality. On the basis of this philosophy a typical figure is the sage sunk in contemplation, trying to look through the veil of unreality. The prophets were not like that. Amos and Micah endeavored to change events in Samaria and Jerusalem; Isaiah and Jeremiah spoke about Assyria and Chaldea. Jesus stood in the Temple court with his arm uplifted in final challenge to his people to align their lives with the purpose of God. According to the prophetic view, history is real.

The people of Jesus' own day, the Greeks and Romans, for the most part thought that history was degeneration. Hesiod and Ovid said that there had been a gold age, then a silver age, less splendid, then a bronze age, more degenerate, and finally an iron age, the most degenerate of all. But the prophets looked forward rather than back; they spent more effort in laboring for the bettering of conditions than in lamenting their worsening. Jesus' disciples were said to have turned the world upside down.

In the modern world some have thought of history as evolution, meaning automatic progress. Samuel Butler said: "Give the world time, an infinite number of epochs, and according to its past and present system, like the coming tide each epoch will advance on each, but so slowly that it can hardly be traced, man's body becoming finer to bear his finer mind, till man becomes not only an angel but an archangel." The prophets and the prophetic Christ, however, do not beguile us with facile optimism; they reckon fully with the sin which corrupts and corrodes human history.

Over against these views of history, we find as distinctive of the prophets and the prophetic Christ the conception that history is a real place of possible but conditional progress. The purpose of God runs through history. The prophets declared that God had made a covenant with his people, and that disobedience to that covenant would bring disaster. As the heir of the prophets and the initiator of the new covenant, Jesus Christ enunciated and made clear anew the intention of God. Man may put his intention in line with the purpose of God, and then make progress. There is no real progress except in a purposeful moving toward the achievement of a goal. "The idea of human progress is only possible," John MacMurray writes, "if human history is conceived as a single action which is realizing an intention."[19] In the thought of the prophets and of Jesus, the intention which is manifest in history is the purpose of God. At any given time, man may or may not put his intention in line with this purpose. If he does not, then there is frustration. The chaos and breakdown which ensue teach that in the long run it is only God's will that will be done. "Whether our intention conforms to the purpose of God or opposes it, we cannot *achieve* anything but the purpose of God."[20] Thus the very idea of progress is most characteristically Christian.

THE GOAL OF HISTORY

What then is the goal of history? There is a clear answer to this in the teaching of Jesus, and it may be seen particularly well in that for which he taught his disciples to pray. When a man prays, he is expressing the deepest desire of his heart; he is aligning his purpose with that about which he is most concerned. Jesus taught men to pray to the heavenly Father:

> *Thy kingdom come,*
> *Thy will be done,*
> *On earth as it is in heaven.*[21]

Without any equivocation the prayer states that the goal of history is the kingdom of God on earth. Again let us seek to understand this against the prophetic background which it sums up and fills full of definitive meaning. In the collection of prophecies which stand in the Old Testament under the name of Isaiah are these descriptions, among others, of what that kingdom will be like:

> And it shall come to pass in the latter days, that the mountain of the Lord's house shall be established on the top of the mountains, and shall be exalted above the hills; and all nations shall flow unto it. . . . And he will judge between the nations, and will decide concerning many peoples; and they shall beat their swords into plowshares, and their spears into pruning-hooks; nation shall not lift up sword against nation, neither shall they learn war any more.[22]
>
> And the wolf shall dwell with the lamb, and the leopard shall lie down with the kid; and the calf and the young lion and the fatling together; and a little child shall lead them. . . . They shall not hurt nor destroy in all my holy mountain; for the earth shall be full of the knowledge of the Lord, as the waters cover the sea.[23]
>
> In that day shall Israel be the third with Egypt and with Assyria, a blessing in the midst of the earth; for that the Lord of hosts hath blessed them, saying, Blessed be Egypt my people, and Assyria the work of my hands, and Israel mine inheritance.[24]

The prophetic hope is for nothing less than a universal human family and an ideal social order. The type of relationship found in the small family group is to be extended until it embraces all mankind. All men, and, in prophetic imagination, even the wild animals too, are to dwell together in peace. There is to be an ideal order of society upon earth. It is for this that we pray when we ask, in the words of Jesus, that the kingdom of God may come and his will be done here as in heaven. It is of this that we sing in words written by Felix Adler:

> *Hail the glorious golden city,*
> *Pictured by the seers of old:*
> *Everlasting light shines o'er it,*
> *Wondrous things of it are told.*
> *Only righteous men and women*
> *Dwell within its gleaming wall;*
> *Wrong is banished from its borders,*
> *Justice reigns supreme o'er all.*

As long as earth's history continues, it has a purpose and meaning. The goal of it and the object of our unwearied striving is the kingdom of God upon earth.

THE TASK IN HISTORY

What does the prophetic Christ want us to do in history? The meaning of history lies in the purpose of God, and the fulfillment of that purpose waits upon human intention being brought into line with the divine intention. As the poem from which we have just quoted goes on:

> *We are builders of that city.*
> *All our joys and all our groans*
> *Help to rear its shining ramparts;*
> *All our lives are building stones.*
> *Whether humble or exalted,*
> *All are called to task divine;*
> *All must aid alike to carry*
> *Forward one sublime design.*

What specifically does Christ want us to do? At least these things. First, repent and believe the gospel. The prophets always uttered a call for repentance. They often proclaimed the imminence of disaster, but they were not only harbingers of doom, they were also heralds of repentance. There was yet hope, if man would change his mind and his way. Jesus likewise, as he began to preach, made his first word the call to repentance. Every acute diagnosis of the problem of our own time comes out to the same conclusion. Schweitzer says: "Our civilization is doomed because it has developed with much greater vigor materially than it has spiritually." D. Elton Trueblood writes: "What we seek is a situation in which we so combine scientific and technical skill with moral and spiritual discipline that the products of human genius shall be used for the welfare of the human race rather than their harm and destruction."[25] We too need to change our mind and our way.

Second, the prophetic Christ wants us to join the fellowship. In an earlier day the prophet Isaiah gathered a small group of disciples, saying, "I will bind up my testimony, and seal my teaching in the heart of my disciples."[26] Jesus did that in a greater and more enduring way, binding together with himself a body of men and women, by baptism, and by the fellowship of the common meal that they ate together, into the beginnings of that organization which marched forward across the years as the church. John Mac-Murray says: "Christianity is only definable in terms of a continuity of intentional action through history."[27] The church represents such a continuity of intentional action in line with the purpose of Christ, reaching down across history and toward the kingdom of God on earth.

In the third place, the prophetic Christ wants us to do missionary work. He sent out his first disciples to preach, and his will continues to impel men to tell his message. If it is to be a universal family which is to constitute the kingdom of God upon earth, this message must be carried everywhere to all people.

As a fourth point, he wants us to recognize the essential human dignity of all men. Only so can a universal family be established. As Elijah took the part of Naboth, the peasant, and as Christ loved the lowliest and the least, so Christianity must recognize the inalienable dignity of every person.

As a fifth consideration, he wants us to have peace. The Old Testament prophet spoke of beating swords into plowshares. How much more potent a transformation if we could turn atomic power for destruction into atomic power for construction. Jesus is called the Prince of peace, and peace is his purpose for his followers.

In the sixth place, he wants us to manifest love toward all. What is meant is no weak, sentimental thing, but something that is strong, intelligent, and good. Love is required of all and toward all, because it is the only principle upon which the universal family and the kingdom of God on earth can be established.

Seventh, he wants us to do whatever work, bear whatever burden, and endure whatever suffering necessary as our part in the task. He himself laid down his life in the fulfillment of his prophetic mission, and he called upon his disciples to take up the cross and follow him. The suffering Servant of God has the right to call others, too, to work which, in such a world as this, can scarcely fail to entail pain. By the cross will come the kingdom.

> *And the work that we have builded*
> *Oft with bleeding hands and tears,*
> *Oft in error, oft in anguish,*
> *Will not perish with our years:*
> *It will live and shine transfigured*
> *In the final reign of right:*
> *It will pass into the splendors*
> *Of the city of the light.*

CHAPTER FOUR

The Apocalyptic Christ

B UT WHAT if the world comes to an end? Jesus certainly came into the world at a period that was specially appropriate for the work he did, and he definitely stands in the history of the world as an unmistakable, unshakable fact. Like the prophets before him, moreover, he appears to have been concerned with the shaping of human history. He reveals the possibility of progress in history in line with the purpose of God and toward the accomplishment of God's kingdom upon earth. As long as history continues he provides a clue to the divine intention that is in it for the establishment of a universal family and an ideal social order on earth. But what if history comes to an end? What if the end of the world takes place? What then about Jesus Christ and all that he teaches?

The end of the world looks decidedly more probable to the ordinary person today than formerly. The atomic end of the world is a very real and terrible possibility. In 1905 a young clerk in Switzerland named Albert Einstein wrote down a formula which read, $E = Mc^2$. Translated, these symbols mean that Energy equals Mass multiplied by a constant squared. The constant is the velocity of light, 186,000 miles or 980,000,000 feet per second. Squared in units of feet this would give a figure of approximately one quintillion. It is by this fantastic figure that the mass of a bit of matter must be multiplied to find the amount of energy to which it is equivalent. Forty years later the implications of the formula became evident to the world when the first atomic bomb fell on Hiroshima. In the same year, 1945, the Smyth report on the use

of atomic energy for military purposes was published. This report
stated that at that time only a fraction of 1 per cent of the possible
total amount of energy was being released, and that if as much as
a few per cent of the possible total amount of energy could be
released, mankind would have the means by which to commit suicide at will. As that development has gone on, it has brought fear
upon the whole earth. What was said a long time ago in II Peter
3:10 looks now like a sober possibility: "the elements will be dis-
solved with fire, and the earth and the works that are upon it will
be burned up." A poet has dedicated these words to Albert Einstein:

> *O dreamer, on the brink*
> *Of time and space, that shrink*
> *Our world to pigmy, now you stand, sad-eyed,*
> *To watch man, blind with fears,*
> *With Samson's scorn of tears,*
> *In fury, hurl the pillars of the world aside.*
>
> *Slain by ourselves, oh then*
> *Will science fashion men?*
> *Our minds are stiffened by a strange new dread.*
> *Along what streams will race*
> *Life's power, when the face*
> *Of man is gone from earth, and lovely earth is dead?*
>
> *Quick, dreamer, bring some word,*
> *Authentic, that shall gird*
> *Our hearts with strength against this self-willed fate!*
> *We know, past time and space,*
> *God moves in love and grace.*
> *His mercy is most stern and most compassionate.*[1]

Astronomically, of course, the end of the world has long been
held probable. According to its spectrum, the sun has been judged
to be already a middle-aged star, and it may be that it will grow
cooler until at last life will be impossible upon earth. Then, in
the words of F. R. Moulton, "the sun, a dead and invisible mass,
will speed on through space with its retinue of lifeless planets."
According to the law of Entropy, the entire universe is running
down like a great clock, and Eddington expects that someday

"time's arrow will cease to point." Or, as Spengler put it, "What the myth of Götterdämmerung signified of old, the irreligious form of it, the theory of Entropy, signifies to-day—world's end as completion of an inwardly necessary evolution." Such theories may require modification in the light of more recent nuclear physics, according to which it is held that the sun's energy comes from the conversion of hydrogen to helium, and that in this atomic process the sun will lose only one ten-thousandth of 1 per cent of its total mass in one hundred and fifty million years. If, however, as some theories anticipate, the rate of radiation were to increase, then the heat upon earth would go up correspondingly. Some think that a temperature of 750 degrees will be reached, the oceans boil away, and everything meet a fiery end. Equally cataclysmic would be the end if, as yet other theories suppose, there is a collision or near collision between heavenly bodies involving our solar system.

In addition to the possibly imminent atomic end and the probably ultimate astronomical end of the world, there is also to be confronted that personal end of the world which is the death of the individual. One of the oldest myths in the world, the Gilgamesh epic of ancient Babylonia, deals with the inevitability of human death. A powerful hero does everything he can to find a way of escape from mortal fate, but in vain. He is told:

> *The life thou seekest thou shalt not find.*
> *When the gods created mankind,*
> *Death they prepared for man,*
> *But life they retained in their hands. . . .*
> *Be merry day and night. . . .*
> *For this is the mission of man.*

Centuries later the book of Ecclesiastes came to the same conclusion: "All are from the dust, and all return to the dust. . . . So I commend mirth; for there is nothing good for man under the sun except to eat, drink, and be merry."[2] The inevitable fate which Gilgamesh and Ecclesiastes contemplated is just as unavoidable today, and the most modern science has no more ability than they to avert this certain end of the world which is the death of the individual person.

It is necessary therefore to raise seriously the question whether the life and teaching of Jesus are oriented simply within a prophetic view of history which looks toward the establishment of an ideal order upon earth, or whether they also have to do with what lies at the end of the world and beyond the end. Was Jesus the apocalyptic Christ?

GENERAL CONSIDERATIONS

The general considerations which point to an affirmative answer to this question include the following. There was a great deal of apocalyptic literature written in the period in which Jesus lived. The period between 200 B.C. and A.D. 100 was one of successive crises, from the persecution by Antiochus IV Epiphanes to the great Jewish war and the actions of the Roman emperors. Old Testament prophecy itself developed at the last increasingly in the direction of apocalyptic. Confronted with the convulsions and catastrophes of the times, men sought to draw back the veil and peer into the inscrutable future to see what was to come. The type of book which they wrote in this endeavor is called an "apocalypse," meaning an uncovering or revealing, and the type of thought represented in it is called "apocalyptic." In the Old Testament the book of Daniel, concerned with the events of the time of Antiochus IV Epiphanes, and in the New Testament the book of Revelation, contemporaneous with Domitian and his persecution of the Christians, are examples of such books. In addition to these two, we know of perhaps thirty or forty other such writings which were circulated but most of which did not attain a place in the final canon of Scriptures. Many of these may be read today in the Apocrypha and Pseudepigrapha. Since such literature was current and such manner of thinking rife precisely in the epoch in which Jesus lived, apocalyptic must be taken into account as a part of the background of his life and a possible part of the framework of his own thought.

Furthermore, apocalyptic expectations certainly surrounded Jesus. His disciples expressed anticipations about the end of the world. For a single revealing example, reference may be made to

Luke 19:11. According to the gospel narrative, Jesus and his followers were at the time on the last journey to Jerusalem. An ominous threat hung over the journey, and yet there was also an atmosphere of expectation. Luke reports that when they came near to the city the disciples "supposed that the kingdom of God was to appear immediately." The kingdom of which they were then thinking could hardly be compared to a seed which would grow slowly to be a great tree, or to a bit of leaven which would gradually leaven an entire lump of dough. It is almost unmistakable that they were expecting that the present order would be broken into abruptly and that the realm of God would come suddenly and gloriously.

Those who formulated the accounts upon which we depend for our knowledge of the life of Jesus also told the story of his life at least partly within an apocalyptic framework. A considerable amount of plainly apocalyptic material is embodied in all three of the synoptic gospels. Interestingly enough, the gospel according to Luke is specially noteworthy in this regard. Although sharing much of the material with Matthew and Mark, there are a number of passages of apocalyptic character which appear only in Luke. The statement just quoted about the disciples supposing that the kingdom of God was to appear immediately is one example, being unparalleled in the other gospels. As Mark, the oldest gospel, was of unusual value in relation to the historicity of Jesus, and Matthew, with its numerous Old Testament quotations, suggested particularly the prophetic nature of his work, so Luke may be taken as a special guide in the study of the apocalyptic aspect of the life and teaching of Jesus.

QUALIFICATIONS

Jesus lived, then, in a world pervaded by apocalyptic interest, his own disciples were animated by apocalyptic hopes, and those who wrote our accounts of his life incorporated in them not a little that is of apocalyptic nature. Do these general considerations indicate that he was himself an apocalyptic figure? Did he speak of apocalyptic matters and regard himself as standing in relation to apocalyptic events?

To these questions an unqualified affirmative answer is given by some who have investigated the problem. Best known of all the scholars who have arrived at such a conclusion is Albert Schweitzer. His famous book, *The Quest of the Historical Jesus,* to which we have already made other reference, comes to a close with a presentation of his own view that the life of Jesus is to be understood in terms of "thoroughgoing eschatology."

In the discussion which follows here, only a qualified affirmative answer will be given to the question at issue, and it is important to make the qualifications explicit. In the following ways Jesus Christ was not an apocalyptic thinker and figure. First, he was not an apocalyptic visionary. It was characteristic of the apocalyptic type of mind to think in visions. The author of the book of Daniel tells of seeing various terrible beasts which signified successive empires of the ancient world. In II Esdras, an eagle is seen rising out of the sea, having twelve wings and three heads. The book of Revelation describes a dragon which is satanic power in the universe, a beast which is the Roman empire, a beast which is the imperial priesthood in Asia Minor, and yet again a beast with the number 666 which is probably Nero. These writers thought in terms of visions. But in the language of Jesus there is none of the fantastic imagery of the typical apocalyptist. He used parables and stories concerning things round about in the world of nature and in the life of man. He was not an apocalyptic visionary.

Again, he was not a prognosticator of times and seasons. Apocalyptic thinkers commonly try to calculate when the end of the world will come. Daniel spoke of "a time and times and half a time,"[3] probably meaning three and one-half years till the kingdom of God would be established. Revised estimates of the time that would elapse may appear in the figures of 1,290 days and 1,335 days which are given at the end of the same book. II Esdras declared: "The life of the world is divided into twelve parts, and nine parts and half of the tenth part are already past, and there are left two parts and half of the tenth part."[4] Revelation evidently returned to the figure given by Daniel, for this book speaks of

1,260 days,[5] which would be three and one-half years of 360 days each. Ever since, these cryptic references, and others, have provided material for those who have sought to determine in advance the time of the end of the world. On the basis of such calculations, men have concluded that the world would come to an end in A.D. 1000, in A.D. 1843, in A.D. 1950, and at many other dates. But Jesus was no prognosticator of seasons and times. He said explicitly, "Of that day or that hour no one knows, not even the angels in heaven, nor the Son, but only the Father."[6]

Further, Jesus was not an advocate of an interim ethic. Albert Schweitzer, who explained the life of Jesus in terms of thoroughgoing eschatology, held that Jesus intended his ethical teachings only for the brief period which would intervene before the end of the world. But Jesus certainly did not say that he meant his words to provide only limited and temporary guidance. Rather he set them forth without qualification as simply the truth, and there is no time limit on the truth.

Yet once again, Jesus was not a proponent of pessimism and fear. Apocalyptic thinking is a characteristic manifestation of a time of crisis. It usually expresses a profound pessimism and represents an abandonment of hope so far as what man can do is concerned. Jesus on the other hand sent his disciples out into the world to work. He summoned them to labor and challenged them to be unafraid.

APOCALYPTIC ASPECTS

If, therefore, we proceed to indicate apocalyptic aspects of the life and teachings of Jesus, the foregoing qualifications must still be kept clearly in mind. The thought of Jesus was not characterized by any of the previously mentioned traits, which commonly come to mind when we speak of apocalyptic. But we may properly call him the apocalyptic Christ for three reasons. First, he does speak about the end of the world. He foresaw and declared the end of the civilization of his own time and his own people. When he and his disciples drew near to the city of Jerusalem on his last visit there at the end of his ministry, the disciples were thinking that the glorious kingdom of God might be at once established and Christ be placed upon his throne of glory, but Jesus himself upon seeing the city wept over it. Later, in the city, he cried out: "O Jerusalem, Jerusalem. . . . How often would I have gathered your children together . . . and you would not! Behold, your house is forsaken."[7] Because of the blind pride of the people in materialistic achievements, because of their empty religion, against which he made a final brave appeal in cleansing the Temple, because of their policies directed toward war, ruin was imminent. The prophecy of that ruin was abundantly fulfilled in A.D. 70, just forty years after Jesus went to the cross. Then and now the apocalyptic Christ signals the end of a civilization that is interested only in materialistic achievement, has an empty religion, and pursues policies of war.

Beyond the end of that immediate civilization Jesus spoke also of the end of the world itself. He did not do this as the apocalyptic writers commonly did, describing it all in fantastic detail, but he certainly did at least allude to it in parabolical language. On one occasion he referred to the return of a master from a marriage feast; the servants would do well to be ready for his return at any hour. Again he spoke of a householder rising up and shutting the door; after it was once closed, it was too late for those on the outside to get in. Yet again he said: "Take heed to yourselves lest your hearts be weighed down with dissipation and drunkenness and cares of this life, and that day come upon you suddenly like a snare; for it will come upon all who dwell upon the face of the whole earth."[8] In every case there is reference to an ultimate consummation of things, to come at a time which men do not know in advance.

In addition to this, Jesus also contemplated that personal end of the world which is the death of the individual. He received the news of the execution of John the Baptist, with whom he had had association, with sorrow; and he saw clearly enough that death by violence was inevitable at the end of the road on which he himself was walking. He witnessed and shared the grief of others who lost members of their families in death. All in all, then, whether in speaking of what would befall the civilization of the day, or in alluding to the consummation of the history of the world, or in facing the death of individuals, Jesus looked forward to an end that was coming.

In the second place, Jesus speaks about what lies beyond the end of the world. He reckons with an end, but he has in view something that is beyond it. To a materialistic philosophy, of course, nothing could lie beyond the end of the world. Since, on the premise of materialism, the external world is all that really exists, when that comes to an end it is the end absolutely. But that is not the case in the teaching of Jesus Christ. On the premises from which he speaks, his teaching could not possibly stop there. To be sure, he does not give any detailed description of what is beyond the end of the world, but he does not fail to give what Amos Wilder, in an article on "The Eschatology of Jesus," calls "an intimation of the ineffable fruition of life."[9] Jesus intimates that there will be an eternal fulfillment of the hope for the kingdom of God. That kingdom is something worth striving for upon earth now, but if this earth comes to an end there will yet be a fulfillment of the kingdom beyond earthly history. He speaks of the time when the king will have the nations before him, some on his right hand and some on his left. Then will he say to those on the right hand, "Come, O blessed of my Father, inherit the kingdom prepared for you from the foundation of the world."[10] When God created the world, he laid a structural foundation for the outworking of his purpose. In the ongoing of history and in the struggles thereof, we are striving in the direction of that goal. But even if that history comes to an end, God's purpose will still not be defeated. His kingdom will be an everlasting kingdom beyond the end of the world. Likewise there will be a fulfillment, beyond the disappointments of life, of the strivings and hopes of the individual. There was a poor man named Lazarus, full of sores. "The poor man died and was carried by the angels to Abraham's bosom."[11] This is Oriental imagery and a Jewish way of speech, but it certainly carries an intimation of an attainment beyond death of some of the things which men struggle for and fail to realize in this life.

In this connection reference may be made to two modern writers.

One is Jean Héring, who published a book in Paris in 1937 on the kingdom of God and its coming. He says that the aspiration for the kingdom of God is aspiration for a kingdom which is neither purely terrestrial nor purely celestial, because it has to be both in order not only to take up into itself the values of creation and history but also to unite both the living and the dead. Furthermore, this aspiration is undergirded by belief in the divine forces which are working toward its effective realization. While such hope is often accompanied by a pessimistic judgment on man and history, it might equally well, says Héring, be combined with "an optimistic conception which places its hope in a progressive purification of humanity up to a relative state of health realizable in this age and leaves to God the responsibility for the great final transfiguration."[12] The "relative state of health realizable in this age," of which Héring speaks, is that better social order to which the prophetic Christ points us; the "great final transfiguration" is the ultimate consummation of which the apocalyptic Christ assures us.

The second contemporary writer is Reinhold Niebuhr, who speaks of the same two sides of Christian hope in his book, *Discerning the Signs of the Times*. "The Christian community prays: 'Thy kingdom come, thy will be done on earth as it is in heaven' and thereby testifies that it believes in the realization of God's will in human history. But it also confesses with St. Paul: 'If in this life only, we had hoped in Christ, we are of all men most miserable,' thereby expressing its understanding of the fact that the Christian hope transcends the limits of history as we know it." Having thus defined these two sides of Christian faith, Niebuhr goes on to express the belief "that an age confronted with so many possibilities of realizing God's will in new dimensions of historic existence, but also confronting so many historic frustrations, is in particular need of the Christian gospel; and requires both the relative-historical, and the final-and-absolute facets of the Christian hope to maintain its sanity and its sense of the meaning of existence."[13]

In the third place, the apocalyptic Christ speaks of his own place in the consummation of the age. He anticipates the end of the world, but he looks to something beyond the end, and in that ultimate consummation he himself will be vindicated. His teachings will stand. "Heaven and earth will pass away, but my words will not pass away."[14] He will be joined again with his disciples. At the Last Supper he ate and drank with them. As he partook of the cup he said, "I tell you I shall not drink again of this fruit of the vine until that day when I drink it new with you in my Father's kingdom."[15] And he will represent humanity in the reception of the kingdom of God. He spoke of himself as the Son of man. In Daniel the phrase personifies the Jewish people, receiving an everlasting kingdom. When Jesus used the title he must have meant that though rejected and slain in his historic mission, he would yet appear in the presence of God as the true representative of Israel, and indeed of all men, to receive on their behalf the kingdom. Indeed there is no more glorious conception of what God is working out in this vast universe than that through history we shall make progress toward his kingdom and at last, if need be beyond the end of history, see the consummation of that kingdom in the glorification of Jesus Christ and the lifting up of him and his way as the everlasting way of truth.

CHAPTER FIVE

The Personal Christ

THE HISTORIC, prophetic, and apocalyptic Jesus is also the personal Christ. Any study of his life is a personal task. Adolf von Harnack once remarked, "Every historical study is an ethical task"; and Albert Schweitzer declared, "There is no historical task which so reveals a man's true self as the writing of a Life of Jesus."[1] Schweitzer went on to point out that the greatest Lives of Jesus were those which were written either with love or with hate, for even hatred of the false trappings with which he had been appareled could animate incisive writing about him. "A personality can only be awakened to life," he said, "by the touch of a personality."[2] When Rudolf Bultmann wrote *Jesus and the Word,* he stated that what he wished to do was to lead his readers not to take a view of history but to experience a highly personal encounter with history.[3] Something of that sort does happen in the study of the life of Jesus. We seek to do it—and it is proper that we should—as scientifically, objectively, and honestly as possible; yet what may have been undertaken with complete detachment turns almost inevitably into a personal encounter.

On the lighter side, this may be illustrated by a story which was told by Forbes-Robertson, the actor. In his London club there was an atheist named Crow, who constantly and vehemently expressed his disbelief in Christ. This continued until one of the members of the club wrote the following quatrain:

We've heard in language highly spiced,
That Crow does not believe in Christ,
But what we're more concerned to know,
Is whether Christ believes in Crow.

We start out to look at Christ but we find that he is looking at us. As P. Carnegie Simpson once put it: "We had thought intellectually to examine him; we find he is spiritually examining us."

In the foregoing three chapters the first three gospels have been referred to as specially suggesting the historic, the prophetic, and the apocalyptic aspects of the life of Christ. Regardless of its special emphasis, each gospel clearly has as its major intention the leading of its readers to a personal meeting with Christ and to faith in him. As the oldest gospel now in our possession, that according to Mark is an unusually valuable historical source. The purpose of the gospel, however, is not just to tell something which happened but to tell what happened in order to evoke faith. It does not close until it has told about a centurion who stood there when Jesus died and was moved to cry, "Truly this man was a son of God."[4] The gospel according to Matthew emphasizes the connections of the life of Jesus with the Old Testament and helps us to see the prophetic Christ, but that gospel does not come to an end until it has expressed the imperative of Jesus, "Go therefore and make disciples of all nations."[5] The gospel according to Luke contains a surprising number of apocalyptic sayings of Jesus which would not otherwise have been preserved, but with all its eschatological sayings it also offers the highly personal story about the One who joined the disciples on the road to Emmaus, and about how they said afterward, "Did not our hearts burn within us while he talked to us on the road?"[6]

Likewise, three books have been specially cited as illustrative of the historic, prophetic, and apocalyptic emphases respectively in the study of the life of Jesus. Each contains in its own way testimony to the fact that the study involves personal encounter. It will be remembered that H. G. Wood asked, "Did Christ really live?" and answered, "Try as we may, we cannot get him out of history." That was the scientific verdict. Then he added, "If we have any sense for reality, we cannot evade his challenge." That was the personal answer. John W. Bowman, in *The Intention of Jesus,* found that it was Jesus' purpose to align himself with the work of the prophets and to form a group which would live the life of the kingdom in fellowship, with himself as its mediator. The personal challenge was central. "In his every word, teaching, and action he laid claim to Lordship over his hearers' minds and hearts. His aphorisms were, many of them, calls to decision; his works, challenges to faith; his parables, demands for insight. Moreover, the decision, faith, and insight unmistakably impinge on himself as the Mediator of the Kingdom experience."[7]

Albert Schweitzer found that Jesus was an apocalyptic figure, "to our time a stranger and an enigma." Yet he concluded *The Quest of the Historical Jesus* with this moving testimony concerning him: "He comes to us as One unknown, without a name, as of old, by the lake-side, He came to those men who knew Him not. He speaks to us the same word: 'Follow thou me!' and sets us to the tasks which He has to fulfil for our time. He commands. And to those who obey Him, whether they be wise or simple, He will reveal Himself in the toils, the conflicts, the sufferings which they shall pass through in His fellowship, and, as an ineffable mystery, they shall learn in their own experience Who He is."[8] Therefore, any study of the life of Christ is a personal task and involves a personal encounter.

The second thing that we must notice is that the personality of Christ looms up above any of the categories in which we try to comprehend him. We seek to understand him as a historical figure, but we know that he is also truly represented in the book title of W. A. Smart, *The Contemporary Christ,* or in that of Walter M. Horton, *Our Eternal Contemporary.* To quote from the former volume: "The contemporary Christ! At times we think that we have him securely shut up in his first century Palestine, and then we discover him walking beside us. The things he says are so simple, and so contemporary, and so impossible. He seems not to fit into this world we know so well; but when we stop long enough to hear what he is saying, we feel that there is no hope for the world unless it will listen to him. He speaks with Palestinian accent the homely things that were true in his little world so long ago, and all at once it dawns on us that they are also the things by which our world must live if it would escape the abyss."[9]

We speak of Jesus as the prophetic Christ, remembering that the people of his day said that he was "one of the prophets."[10] But we know that that opinion concerning his identity did him scant justice, since he was the fulfillment of that for which the prophets hoped. The prophets characteristically introduced their utterances, "Thus saith the Lord,"[11] but he spoke directly, "I say to you."[12] He was not just one of the prophets, but the Messiah for whom the prophets were looking. We call him the apocalyptic Christ, and yet his teachings and character quite exceed the limits which we customarily associate with the apocalyptic idea. Thus it must be said that Jesus is the personal Christ in the sense that he is a personality who transcends the limits of any of these frameworks in which we try to place him and through which we try to understand him.

CHRIST AND GOD

Then we may go further and say that the personal Christ is a revelation of a personal God. In this connection also we may cite an ancient gospel and a modern book. The gospel according to John comes particularly to mind. It was undoubtedly written out of long and profound meditation upon the meaning and inner significance of the life of Christ, and it gives a penetrating statement of what that meaning was. In it, in John 14:9, Jesus says, "He who has seen me has seen the Father." Can we set alongside that any modern book? One that may be suggested is by John Knox, entitled *The Man Christ Jesus*. Here is a portion of the conclusion of this book: "No reader of the New Testament can escape the impression that within the primitive Christian community, whose life the documents reflect, an event of incalculable magnitude had occurred, an event of such magnitude that those who witnessed it could confidently believe that it was nothing less than God's supreme disclosure of himself to men. The center of this event was the character and career of the man Christ Jesus. In him God had acted to redeem those who would receive him, and in the community which had been formed about him, and of which he was the living center, that redemption was offered to all mankind. This was the faith of the early church. . . . and the faith rests firmly upon what men had actually found in Jesus, and find there still."[13] Or, to put it in another way, we may say with Rufus M. Jones, "If we are to suppose . . . that the universe in its loftiest aspects shows 'a spiritual adventure' already in process, we shall find the clearest evidences of such an adventure in the revelation of love which breaks through the life and death of Christ."[14]

CHRIST AND THE KINGDOM

Once again we may state that the personal Christ offers us the kingdom of God as a personal possession in the present. Inevitably in consideration of the life of Jesus we have spoken often of that kingdom of God for which he taught men to pray and for which he laid down his own life. As the prophetic Christ, Jesus interprets and shapes history as progress toward the kingdom which will be an ideal social order with a universal family of mankind upon earth. As the apocalyptic Christ, he speaks about an eternal kingdom which is beyond the limits of history. If the world comes to an end, there is yet a kingdom of God beyond the world, and if life comes to an end, as soon or late it must, beyond death there is an everlasting life. But the kingdom of God which is the goal of prophetic striving may be yet a thousand years away, or perchance a million. And the kingdom of God which apocalyptic hope glimpses is beyond the end of history and beyond the mysterious portal of death, a portal that is passed only at God's summons. Is the kingdom of God then only something that is far ahead in history, or that is beyond history and beyond death? No. The kingdom of God is also something that is present here and now. C. H. Dodd interprets the parables of Jesus in terms of "realized eschatology." With the coming of Christ, the kingdom of God has already come. As Dodd puts it: "The teaching of Jesus is not an ethic for those who expect the speedy end of the world, but for those who have experienced the end of this world and the coming of the Kingdom of God."[15] Jesus himself indeed said: "If it is by the finger of God that I cast out demons, then the kingdom of God has come upon you."[16] "Blessed are the eyes which see what you see! For I tell you that many prophets and kings desired to see what you see, and did not see it, and to hear what you hear, and did not hear it."[17] In a real sense the kingdom of God was inaugurated with the life of Christ. It is a possible personal possession right now in the present. As Jesus says, "The kingdom of God is in the midst of you."[18] Even while we continue to strive toward that "far-off divine event, to which the whole creation moves," and even while we strengthen our hearts in the assurance that those who have died have not been lost but carried into the presence of God himself and into his everlasting kingdom, we can also experience the kingdom as a present personal possession.

CHRIST AND PERSONS

Once more, we may say that the personal Christ is a companion of persons on the pathway of history. Here we are, striving for that distant goal of the kingdom of God on earth. Here we are, anticipating that even if the end of the world break in upon us sometime, as certainly it must individually, out beyond are the high towers of the eternal city of God. Here we are, in the midst of the struggles and endeavors of the present time, daring also to believe that the kingdom is present even now if we can only see it, and that Christ is even now a personal companion on the pathway of the present time. In the gospel according to John it is written: "I will not leave you desolate; I will come to you."[19] Again and again some lone wanderer in a desolate place of earth, or in a desolating experience of life, has known that this is true, that this spiritual reality of the universe which is best revealed in Jesus Christ is a personal comforting presence. Sir Ernest Shackleton and his two companions, Crean and Worsley, made their hazardous way across the frozen wastes of Antarctica not only to save their own lives but to rescue their marooned companions. They did not say anything about it at the time, but when the three men talked of it later, as Shackleton tells in his book, *South,* they confessed in common to the feeling that many times they had been not three but four. T. Howard Somervell was one of five men to go above 28,000 feet on Mount Everest. He said, "I have often felt the presence of a Companion on the mountains who is not of our earthly party of climbers." Francis Thompson was in desperate need in London, poor, wretched, and sick. He wrote, and the words were found among his papers when he died:

> *Yea, in the night, my Soul, my daughter,*
> *Cry, clinging heaven by the hems:*
> *And lo, Christ walking on the water,*
> *Not of Gennesaret, but Thames!*[20]

CHAPTER SIX

The Light of the World[1]

THE EARLIEST parts of the New Testament tell little or nothing of the birth of Jesus. Paul says only that he was "descended from David according to the flesh."[2] Mark begins directly with the opening of his public ministry when he was a grown man. It is evident that at the outset his followers were chiefly concerned with what he did in his period of active work. Later New Testament sources, however, notably Matthew and Luke, contain accounts of his birth. When men formulated these accounts they did so largely in the form and spirit of poetry. It is hardly possible any longer to demonstrate, as some have undertaken to do, that certain of the records are derived from Joseph, others directly from Mary. Vincent Taylor concludes a book devoted to the discussion of the matter by remarking that if the tradition of the birth is to be taken as it stands it means another foothold for faith in history, but that even if it must be regarded as a legend it shows the remarkable faith of the Jewish Christians who offered to Jesus the tribute of telling such a story of his birth. "If, in the end," says Taylor, "we must call poetry what they called fact, it will not be because we are strangers to their faith."[3]

While the stories may be poetry, they may still tell us the truth. Indeed poetry sometimes conveys truth more successfully than prose. It represents a measure of intuition and a manner of expression adapted to the apprehension and utterance of wonderful things. At all events, the poetry in which the narrative of the birth of Jesus is enshrined is congruous in spirit with what we know of the character of the one of whom it tells. Contrasting with the crudities in many of the birth stories which appear in the myths of the gods in ancient Mesopotamia and Egypt and in the legends surrounding the lives of religious founders in the Orient is the chaste and devout spirit which pervades the New Testament accounts. The modern poet, Marya Zaturenska, tells of the Messenger who brought her her message and of how she shapes her style that it may be as pure as he.

> *For that prized messenger,*
> *Who for a little while*
> *Revealed his haunted face,*
> *I write, I shape my style.*
>
> *And let it be as pure*
> *As that unearthly brow*
> *Whose words I study now*
> *And keep secure.*[4]

Even so, those ancient authors whose poems on Jesus' birth are in our New Testament wrote words which reflect the spirit of their subject.

To the understanding of what is phrased in poetry it is necessary to bring as much as we can of a poetic spirit. It is proper to respond with a sense of wonder, a quickened imagination, and kindled emotions.

STARLIGHT

In the second chapter of Matthew the story of the star of Bethlehem is told. Wise men saw a star in the East and, guided by its light, came to worship Christ at his birth. While the story may be a legend like the stories of stars which appeared when Mithridates and Alexander Severus were born, for example, it nevertheless fits very appropriately into the situation of the time. In the Greek text the wise men are called Magi. Strictly, these were a tribe of priests among the Medes and Persians, to which Zoroaster belonged. In ancient times they had a reputation for great learning, and Pythagoras is said to have studied with them, while Plato wished to. More broadly, the term may have been intended to connote Babylonian astrologers in general. While we call their learning astrology and recognize that it was much used for purposes of divination, yet actually it included a great deal of genuine astronomical knowledge. In ancient Babylonia lists of stars were drawn up, the constellations were plotted, and the movements of the planets were followed. The Venus tablets of Ammisaduqa, for example, are well known to archeologists: they represent tabulated observations of the planet Venus made by the Babylonian king Ammisaduqa, and have a high degree of accuracy. Not only was study of the heavens and a searching there for portents of what was to happen upon earth perfectly familiar in that time; there was also a widespread expectation in the East, deriving ultimately perhaps from Jewish Messianic speculation, that a universal king and deliverer would arise in the West. Some students, therefore, have judged that the Star of Bethlehem was an actual celestial phenomenon and have identified it, for example, with a conjunction of Jupiter and Saturn which took place about the beginning of our era. At any rate, ever since this poetic and beautiful account was first told, a star has been a symbol of Christ. In him was seen a fulfillment of the prophecy in Numbers 24:17: "There shall come forth a star."

There are indeed many ways in which the coming and the life of Christ are like starlight. The stars are signals to us of the glory of God, and so too is the life of Jesus. Much of the Bible has come to us out of the wilderness country of the Near East, where the air is particularly clear and the stars incredibly near and bright. There, too, men took time to think about their meaning. As a result of such reflection, it is written in the nineteenth Psalm:

> *The heavens declare the glory of God;*
> *And the firmament showeth his handiwork.*

Or in the stately paraphrase of Joseph Addison:

> *The spacious firmament on high,*
> *With all the blue ethereal sky,*
> *And spangled heavens, a shining frame,*
> *Their great Original proclaim.*

When Michael Pupin was president of the American Association for the Advancement of Science, the distinguished immigrant recalled his boyhood in Serbia. There he often herded grazing oxen by night, and looking up at the stars he was enchanted by their brilliance. He imagined that the light of the stars was a message from God telling the hour of the night and the direction of the coming dawn. As a mature scientist he devoted himself to a search for an answer to the question, What is light? He found that light was a series of electronic pulses coming through space from the sun and stars. These tiny impulses stimulate the nerves of the eye which carry messages to the brain, and there the soul deciphers and interprets their meaning. "And the more I think of it as a scientist," said Pupin, "the more do I feel that those gleams of light from the quiet stars which fell upon my eyes as I tended the oxen, were really messages to the soul, declaring the glory of God."

If the stars signal God's glory, so too does the life of Christ, more remarkable than all the stars of the sky.

The stars burn with incandescent fervor, and so too did the life of Christ. Astronomers have measured the temperatures of the stars and reported surface temperatures ranging from 3,000 to 30,000 degrees centigrade, interior temperatures from 30,000,000 degrees to 100,000,000 degrees. It is in the millions of degrees of temperature in the sun that the process of fusion that transforms hydrogen into helium takes place, the process which is now believed to be the secret of the sun's enormous energy. Does the radiance of Christ come, like starlight, out of the incandescent fervor of his life? Indeed it does! Some of his disciples have manifested something of it too. Once I heard Dr. Walter Judd, then a China missionary, speak in an impassioned appeal concerning China. Afterward a newspaper writer described the address as "illuminated almost to incandescence." Henry Martyn arrived in Calcutta, where he was to work for seven brief but fruitful years in missionary service. Upon his arrival his words were prophetic, "Now let me burn out for God." These men would be the first to testify that the life of Jesus was yet more incandescent in its fervor.

The stars illuminate the journey of life and point it to the skies.

There is a saying, "A star gleamed in the window of heaven like a candle to remind the lonely that God is at home." The life of Jesus is our best reminder, shining in the firmament of human life, that back of it all and above it all is God.

The stars shine most brightly when it is darkest. When the garish lights of the city are near at hand, the stars are dimmed, even the moon seems less brilliant. On some high, lonesome place where it is utterly dark all around, the stars are seen shining in all their splendor. Jesus' life shines out most brightly of all against the dark background of tragedy in which it came to a close. Sometimes only when we ourselves experience solitude, loneliness, or sorrow, do we in that gloom see that he is with us.

The stars provide an intimation of immortality. They cannot even be seen while it is daytime, but after the sun goes down the stars come out. Is life like a daytime? When the brightness of the day is upon us, it dazzles us and makes us unable to see the infinite reaches of existence. When the darkness of death shuts down, a world now undreamed of may burst into view. So, too, Christ provides for man an intimation of his immortality.

SUNLIGHT

If the story of the birth of Christ in Matthew suggests that he is like starlight, the story in Luke suggests that he is like sunlight. In the first chapter of this gospel is the hymn of Zechariah. Zechariah was the father of John the Baptist, and he is pictured as uttering the words of the hymn on the occasion when his small son was eight days old and was given the name John. In it he spoke of how the child would go before the Christ and prepare the way for him.

> *Yea, and thou, child, shalt be called the prophet of the*
> *Most High:*
> *For thou shalt go before the face of the Lord to make ready*
> *his ways . . .*
> *Because of the tender mercy of our God,*
> *Whereby the dayspring from on high shall visit us.*[5]

The coming of Christ was like the arrival of the dayspring. He is like sunlight, and that is what brings the morning. His coming was like the burst of dawn over the eastern hills. The marvel of the morning is one of the most wonderful things anyone ever experiences. Climbing in the mountains, starting in the dead of night, how eagerly one watches for the first faint lightening of the sky in the east; how gladly one welcomes the dawn when the sun comes above the horizon. Sunrise in the desert has been described in a tone poem in the "Grand Canyon Suite" written by Ferde Grofé. One stands in the Painted Desert in the darkness. Then there is the first faint stirring of life as the night draws toward its end and the morning begins to approach. Then the light begins to come, faintly, then more and more brightly, until in a glorious paean, in a great crescendo, the sun rises.

Jesus Christ is like that, sunrise for the earth. When the morning comes and the sun rises, it seems appropriate to think of him. "When morning gilds the skies, my heart awaking cries, May Jesus Christ be praised!" His own coming was like the coming of morning in the history of the world. Long ago in western civilization it was decided to mark the dividing point in chronology at the birth of Jesus, and hence we date B.C., "before Christ," and A.D., Anno Domini, "in the year of the Lord." Does that division and what it connotes still hold good? Kenneth S. Latourette, one of our most thoroughgoing historians, has condensed the results of extended researches in a book entitled *Anno Domini*. In it he speaks of the life of Jesus and answers the question we have just raised like this:

> Measured by its fruits in the human race, that short life has been the most influential ever lived on this planet. . . . The impress of that life, far from fading with the passing centuries, has deepened. Never has Jesus had so wide and so profound an effect upon humanity as in the past three or four generations. Through him millions of individuals have been transformed and have begun to live the kind of life which he exemplified. Through him movements have been set in motion which have made in society for what mankind believes to be its best—in the inward transformation of human lives, in political order, in the production and distribution of goods to meet the physical needs of men, in healing physical

ills, in the relations between races and between nations, in art, in religion, and in the achievements of the human intellect. Gauged by the consequences which have followed, the birth, life, death, and resurrection of Jesus have been the most important events in the history of man. Measured by his influence, Jesus is central in the human story. The chronology which reckons time by the categories Before Christ and Anno Domini is correct. Far from outmoding it, accumulating human experience only confirms the insight displayed in its adoption.[6]

Sunlight also seems to multiply itself. Out in Palestine, where Jesus lived, the Syrian sun is specially brilliant and radiant. Adolf Deissmann wrote a book entitled *Licht vom Osten,* literally "Light from the East." In it he describes the Syrian sunlight: how when a beam of it falls into a room, "it begins to dawn, to glitter and to move; the one beam seems to double itself, to multiply itself tenfold." In a dark room on the shore of the Sea of Galilee, I have opened the door after sunrise just a crack and have seen this radiant light flooding into the room and seeming to multiply itself indeed, until all the room was light and bright. Christ is like that, for coming into the world the light of his life has multiplied itself and spread everywhere.

Sunlight reveals and thereby judges. It was anticipated that when the Christ came, he would be the judge of the world. Many people pictured this in a way derived from Daniel, and anticipated a throne upon the clouds and the last great Assize. Jesus did not judge men in that manner. Nevertheless he did judge men simply by his coming. As it is put in the gospel according to John: "And this is the judgment, that the light has come into the world, and men loved darkness rather than light, because their deeds were evil."[7] Sunlight reveals pitilessly—and thereby judges more inexorably than any artificial judgment possibly can. The sunlight that is Christ has been, ever since, a judgment in the world.

Sunlight heals and cleanses and promotes growth. What a pitiful thing is a plant that grows in the darkness, pale; or a little child that lives in the slums, pallid; or an Indian huddled in his windowless hogan, the prey of tuberculosis. What a good thing is the sunlight that encourages growth, cleanses, and makes healthy.

Watch a rose in the morning, with the bud folded tight. Then as the sun shines upon it and the hours go on, it opens out. Life has been like that in the presence of Christ. He has been sunlight in the life of mankind. The words of Henry van Dyke apply to him as to God: "Hearts unfold like flowers before Thee, opening to the sun above." Latourette describes the universal influence of Jesus around the world, bringing out the best in man everywhere:

> In man is something which responds to Jesus, and . . . this something is what man believes to be his own highest and best. . . . When once it knows him, that best in man welcomes Jesus and is quickened and reinforced by him. This is true regardless of race and culture. Again and again, in many ages and nations and tribes, and in various states of civilization, through contact with Jesus men and women have borne what Paul calls the fruits of the Spirit. These fruits have appeared among the Eskimos of the Arctic, among the Patagonians of South America, among the Hottentots of South Africa, among the aborigines of the Pacific Islands, and among the finest products of Japanese, Chinese, Hindu, and European civilizations. As one looks at some of his friends in present-day Scandinavia and recalls their strong gentleness, their unselfish love, and their fineness of perception, and then remembers that their ancestors were the ruthless pirates who ravaged western Europe and that the change has come primarily through the influence of Jesus, he realizes afresh that in every race, even the most unlikely, there is that which is akin to Jesus and which through contact with him comes to fruition.[8]

LAMPLIGHT

In the gospel according to John, Jesus himself says, "I am the light of the world."[9] The occasion on which he made this declaration was at the feast of Tabernacles. This feast commemorated the time when the Israelites dwelt in tents in the wilderness. One feature of the observance was the brilliant illumination of the court of the women in the Temple, perhaps in memory of the Pillar of Fire which led the people in the wilderness. Four golden lampstands were there, and at the close of the first day of the feast the worshipers went into the court to light these, and doubtless many other lights as well. On every night throughout the feast the illumination was probably continued. The Talmud declares that there was not a courtyard in Jerusalem that was not illumined by the light, and that a woman could sift wheat by it, it was so bright.[10]

Since the chief source of light at this time was lamps, it may be supposed that lamplight was primarily in mind in a statement about light made on this occasion. Jesus Christ, who is like starlight and sunlight, is therefore also like lamplight. Lamplight is the illumination of the home of the humble. It shines upon the woman sifting her wheat, the man working at his trade, the child at play. Lamplight is that by which one searches for what is lost. "What woman, having ten silver coins, if she loses one coin, does not light a lamp and sweep the house and seek diligently until she finds it?"[11] Lamplight is that by which one is led along the path. It shines scarcely far enough for more than the next step, but when that step is taken the way can be seen yet a little farther. In all of these ways Jesus himself is like lamplight, entering the homes of the humblest, seeking out the least and last and lost, and saying, "He who follows me will not walk in darkness, but will have the light of life."[12]

Part II: The Message of Jesus

CHAPTER SEVEN

Three Conceptions of Religion

WHEN JESUS began to teach, what kind of religion did he present? A clue to an answer may be found in the statement in Matthew 5:20: "Unless your righteousness exceeds that of the scribes and Pharisees, you will never enter the kingdom of heaven."

LEGALISM

The first kind of religion, than which ours must be better if we are to enter the kingdom of heaven, is that of the scribes. To this kind it is customary to give the name of legalism. It represents a conception of religion primarily as laws to be obeyed. Here are some of the factors in how this conception originated. Law is found throughout the Old Testament. According to the Old Testament, God and man can and do have a relationship to one another, and a covenant can exist between them. Where there is such a covenant it carries with it promises from God, and it also involves requirements upon man. These requirements are the things man must do if the promises of God are to be fulfilled.

When God made a covenant with Noah, he promised him, through the sign of the rainbow in the sky, that he was not going to destroy the earth with a flood ever again. And he required of Noah that he eat meat of the fashion that we call "kosher." When God made an agreement with Abraham, he promised Abraham that he would give him descendants as numerous as the sands of the seashore, and required of him that he and those descendants obey the law of circumcision. When he made a covenant with the children of Israel at Mount Sinai, God promised those wandering slaves that he would go with them and help them to be a nation. He required of them that they promise to abide by his commandments—the Ten Commandments and other laws. Thus, obeying God's law is man's part if God's promises are to be fulfilled.

In the experience of crisis, it was perceived more clearly than before how important obedience is. In 721 B.C. the Northern Kingdom was overwhelmed by the military might of Assyria. In 587 B.C. Judah was destroyed by the military power of Chaldea. The prophets who were living at that time said that these catastrophes had come because the people had not obeyed God's law. They had not lived up to their part of the agreement with God and he could not bless them unless and until they did. When they returned from the bitter punishment of the exile, therefore, they felt more strongly than ever that it was absolutely necessary to keep the law, and the tendency toward legalism was much strengthened. It was then that the scribes began to emerge into greatest importance as a class of professional scholars devoted to the study and exposition of the law.

There are very good features about this kind of religion, which is based upon recognition of the laws of God. For one thing, it makes plain to the ordinary man what religion is and what he is expected to do. There can be no doubt that Jewish legalism developed out of a deep and sincere concern to really know the will of God and to have it written out so plainly that no one could be in doubt as to what he should do. In contrast to some of our modern preaching, which consists of a vague exhortation to a generalized goodness, there is in legalism an unequivocalness of statement that is refreshing. Without doubt many a person, confused and perplexed by all kinds of modern opinions on every subject, is profoundly grateful that at some critical juncture in his life he has had come to him the word of the law: "thou shalt"—"thou shalt not." Here is something that is definite, by which to be guided, and onto which to hold.

Furthermore, this way of looking at religion recognizes the place of duty in our faith. Duty, as Wordsworth put it, is the "stern Daughter of the Voice of God." Religion is not worth very much if it ever lets that conviction evaporate.

Nevertheless, as the kind of religion of which we are speaking developed it came to be what we call legalism, and in legalistic religion there are dangers and evils. In the system of legalism, life may become cluttered up with laws which are out of date. Consider the law about kosher meat, which was first laid upon Noah, according to the Old Testament. There are those who still feel that to abide by that law is one of the most important things in life. But even among the Jewish people themselves there are now many of liberal thought who feel that the dietary laws of the Old Testament are no longer binding. Once upon a time, they believe, these laws may have been of importance. Probably they had an empirical basis and did conduce to health. But now they are no longer relevant, and so they can properly be left behind. A legalist, however, can hardly leave any law behind and hence is apt to keep his life overcrowded and confused with out-dated laws.

Furthermore, he always has to keep making new laws to cover new circumstances. New problems arise, and one cannot know what to do about the new problems until he gets the new law on the subject. Consequently the legalist tends to get so many laws, constantly increasing, that it is difficult to know which are important and which are unimportant. He may conclude that all are equally binding. Rabbi Judah said, "Be heedful of a light precept as of a grave one." Thus life becomes loaded with a multiplicity of laws and rules.

Also, in legalism the danger is encountered that one will not have the law book at hand when one needs it most. Suddenly he confronts a problem and if he does not have the code there to consult he does not know what to do. Not only that; in legalism one may be tempted to fulfill the letter of the law and disregard the spirit. It is sometimes possible to perform every outward requirement but to produce a result precisely the opposite of the actual intent of the law.

Once again, in a legalistic system, man may be made either rebellious or self-righteous. He may come to feel that there are so many laws that he cannot possibly keep them all, therefore why try to keep any of them? The "people of the land" in Jesus' day were like that. Feeling that it was an impossible assignment, they simply abandoned the effort to keep the law at all. Others, in effect, checked off in their book of rules the various items of their own exemplary conduct. "Thou shalt"—they checked off where they had done those things. "Thou shalt not"—they checked off those too. They had not done the things that it said not to—so they concluded that they were perfect. A man like that stood up in the Temple to pray, and his prayer was little save a boast. He thanked God that he was not like other men. He had fasted and paid his tithes. He had done what the law said. Hence he was righteous, while those who had not done it were sinners. Actually he was self-righteous.

The unfortunate outcome of legalism may be illustrated with regard to one single matter, that of keeping the Sabbath day. In the Ten Commandments it is stated that man must remember the Sabbath day to keep it holy; six days he is to labor, on the seventh day he is not to do any work. As time went along, men felt the need of finding out exactly what might be done on the Sabbath day and what might not be done, in order to obey this commandment. So the students of the law developed more and more derivative rules to tell people exactly what to do and what not to do on the Sabbath. So many rules came into existence that they now fill an entire large-sized volume in the Talmud. Here are some of the items. How far may one walk on the Sabbath day? A legalist has to know. If he takes a step beyond the limit he is breaking the law. It was concluded that one may walk two thousand cubits, roughly three-fifths of a mile, on the Sabbath day and still be keeping the commandment. But if one goes farther than that, then he has broken the law. But an ingenious method was devised for getting around the rule if necessary. The day before, one goes that far from home and puts there a piece of personal property. Residence is clearly established where property is. On the Sabbath day he walks that far, and then, taking a fresh start, goes three-fifths of a mile beyond. No law has then been broken. Thus the system eventuated in absurdity and subterfuge.

May knots be tied on the Sabbath day? It was decided that there were some knots which could be tied on the Sabbath without breaking the law, and others which, if tied, constituted breaking of the law. What about a man with a sore throat? May he use vinegar for relief? The conclusion was that he may if he only swallows a small amount to make his throat feel better; but if he gargles with it, that is doing work and is forbidden. May a person sick unto death call for a physician to attend him? Fortunately, in this case it was decided that it would be permissible. But in the case of a man who had suffered a fracture, he might not call a physician on the Sabbath day, and a man who had sprained his hand or foot might not even pour cold water over it. Furthermore, there was a law that a woman might not look in a mirror on the Sabbath day, lest she see a gray hair and be tempted to pull it out, which would be doing work. And two of the most famous rabbis, Hillel and Shammai, had a strenuous argument and maintained different sides on the question whether an egg that a hen laid on the Sabbath could be eaten. The problem was, did the hen do work in laying the egg? If so, the egg was unclean and could not be partaken of!

This is the absurd kind of thing into which legalism degenerates. It is not only something that was known two thousand years ago; it also existed in early America. The first Sunday law that was passed in America is to be found as a part of the "Articles, Laws, and Orders, Divine, Politique, and Martial, for the Colony in Virginia; first established by Sir Thomas Gates, Knight, Lieutenant-General, the 24th of May 1610." The law reads: "Every man and woman shall repair in the morning to the divine service and sermons preached upon the sabbath day, and in the afternoon to divine service, and catechizing, upon pain for the first fault to lose their provision and the allowance for the whole week following; for the second, to lose the said allowance and also to be whipped; and for the third to suffer death." It is good and desirable for people to go to church, but only because they want to, not because if they miss one Sunday they are going to lose their allowance for the following week, if they miss twice they are going to be whipped, and if they miss three times they are going to be executed.

That was the end to which the legalistic ordering of life came, a dismal end indeed. That is why, unless our righteousness exceeds that of the scribes and that of any legalistic system, we will never enter the kingdom of heaven.

DOGMATISM

The second kind of religion, than which ours must be better if we are to enter the kingdom of heaven, is that of the Pharisees. In one aspect at least we may define this as dogmatism. According to dogmatism, religion is primarily doctrines to be believed. The Pharisees were committed to certain doctrines which they regarded as established and of which they were the protagonists. They held definite beliefs on the providence of God, the freedom of man, the immortality of the soul, the resurrection of the body, future retribution, angels, spirits, and the coming Messiah. On all of these points they entered into controversy with those who thought otherwise than themselves, most particularly the Sadducees. It is therefore not surprising that standard works on the Pharisees speak of their dogmatics.

Like legalism, dogmatism was not limited to a time two thousand years ago. Christians as well as Jews have been dogmatic, perhaps more so. Theologians, both of the Roman Catholic church and of the Protestant churches, have often set forth positive opinions and expected acquiescence in them on the part of others.

The origin of dogmatism is of course not difficult to understand. Religion is clearly belief as well as duty. Obviously then it is necessary to know what to believe. To answer the question of what to believe, dogmas are set forth. A dogma is an accepted opinion; a definite and authoritative tenet; a doctrine formally stated and authoritatively proclaimed. Likewise arise creeds. These are statements of beliefs. Written in Latin, as many of them were, they often began with the word *Credo,* "I believe." From this we derive the noun "creed." Similarly we have catechisms. In them there is a series of questions, with brief answers which may be memorized. For example: Question—What is the end of man? Answer—The end of man is to glorify God and enjoy him forever. Thus by a natural and understandable development we get the dogmas and creeds and catechisms of a dogmatic religion.

About dogmatism, as about legalism, there are very good features. Here faith is made a definite thing, as duty is in legalism. People want answers to the problems which perplex them. Dogmatic religion does not hesitate to give answers. There is a battle of ideas going on in the world. Dogmatic religion enters that battle, committed to a clear-cut set of convictions.

But in dogmatic religion there are certain dangers. This kind of religion tends toward arrogance. If we are in possession of the answers to our questions, we may no longer be humble seekers, questing, but ones who know and who know that they know. Dogmatic religion tends not to honor but to castigate doubt, yet there may be "more faith in honest doubt . . . than in half the creeds." Dogmatism tends toward pride in ability to quote authoritative writings and therewith controvert opponents, but as Shakespeare remarked, "The devil can cite Scripture for his purpose." Dogmatic religion tends to emphasize intellectual belief, but concerning belief alone James said: "You believe that God is one; you do well. Even the demons believe—and shudder."[1]

Examples of the unfortunate outworking of dogmatic religion are not hard to find. In A.D. 325 there was a great controversy within Christendom. The leader of one party, Arius, was banished, and died in exile before he could be restored to the fellowship of Christianity. The leader of the other party, Athanasius, was sent five times into exile. Thus men came to hate each other because of their dogmatism. In A.D. 1054 the representatives of the Roman Catholic church visited Constantinople and deposited in the great cathedral of Hagia Sophia a bull of excommunication which excluded from Christian fellowship, as far as they were concerned, the head of all the eastern Christians and condemned him, "along with all heretics, together with the devil and his angels." The great schism thus marked has never been healed. In A.D. 1553 Servetus was burned at the stake. Through centuries the tortures of the Inquisition were continued. All of these deeds were motivated by dogmatic religion working at its worst. Our religion and righteousness must exceed that of any and all such dogmatism and Pharisaism if we are to enter the kingdom of heaven.

ENTHUSIASM

What is the righteousness which goes beyond both legalism and dogmatism? While no one word may suffice to comprehend what Jesus taught, we may venture to call his the religion of enthusiasm. It is religion in which the fundamental thing is not law to be obeyed, nor doctrine to be intellectually assented to, but love to be experienced and shared.

This kind of religion assuredly found its chief origin in the world in the life of Jesus Christ. He lived in the strong assurance of the love of God and in the constant expression of that love. God is certainly the moral order of the universe. He is certainly the wisdom that has created this universe. But according to the life and teaching of Jesus, God is also love. In the life of Christ men have seen what that love is like, and have felt the radiance of it.

When religion is the enthusiasm of a life to be lived like Christ's life, in the experience and sharing of the divine love, then both law and belief come into their proper positions. Law has a place. The followers of Jesus are not called to antinomianism. They do not feel that the moral law is to be dispensed with. They keep the law, but do so in love. They feel that it is a light and easy and natural thing to do this, rather than an onerous burden. This attitude was already manifest in certain passages in the Old Testament. The Psalmist expressed it when he cried, "Oh how love I thy law!" and when he said, "Thy statutes have been my songs in the house of my pilgrimage," or as Moffatt translates, "Thy statutes are my songs, as I wander through the world."[2] The law of God is not a burden but a blessing if we understand that it comes from his love. Furthermore, the followers of Jesus go beyond the law because they perform acts which no one could possibly be constrained to do by any law on the subject.

As for belief, it was never intended, according to the teaching of Jesus, to be an arid intellectual assent to the proposition that God exists, but rather a personal and living trust in and devotion to him. "Faith" is the word which both Jesus and Paul use for this attitude, and what it connotes is clear when Paul speaks in Galatians of "faith working through love."[3] Devoted trust in God expresses itself in relationships of good will to men. The followers of Jesus live thus, in the experience and sharing of love.

The nature of the religion of enthusiasm is suggested in Gilbert K. Chesterton's contrast of Christian virtues to natural ones. The pagan or natural virtues, he says, are sad virtues; the Christian are gay and exuberant, involving paradox. "Justice consists in finding out a certain thing due to a certain man and giving it to him. Temperance consists in finding out the proper limit of a particular indulgence and adhering to that. But charity means pardoning what is unpardonable, or it is no virtue at all. Hope means hoping when things are hopeless, or it is no virtue at all. And faith means believing the incredible, or it is no virtue at all. . . . Hope is the power of being cheerful in circumstances which we know to be desperate. . . . There is a state of hope which belongs to bright prospects and the morning; but that is not the virtue of hope. The virtue of hope exists only in earthquake and eclipse."[4]

Li Hung Chang, a Chinese leader, contrasted Christianity and Confucianism. He declared that he honored Christianity but preferred Confucianism. It was possible, he found, to be a good Confucianist; the rules of the religion could actually be obeyed. But one could not be a good Christian; the ideals of Christ were beyond attainment.[5]

Schubert wrote instructions for the conductor in the manuscript of one of his symphonies. At one place he marked in the margin, "as loud as possible." A little farther on he wrote, "still louder."[6] Like that, Christianity calls always for something more. Peter asked if he should forgive his brother as many as seven times, and Jesus told him seventy times seven. Jesus himself went to the cross and not only was crucified but also prayed that God would forgive those who had done this to him. Thus there is always something more, always a plus, in Christianity.

L. P. Jacks wrote a book entitled *The Lost Radiance of the*

Christian Religion. "Christianity," he declared, "is the most encouraging, the most joyous, the least repressive and the least forbidding of all the religions of mankind. There is no religion which throws off the burden of life so completely, which escapes so swiftly from sad moods, which gives so large a scope for the high spirits of the soul, and welcomes to its bosom with so warm an embrace those things of beauty which are joys for ever. The Christian Religion has arduous phases. . . . But the end of it all is . . . an ascent into the heights and not a lingering in the depths."[7] Christianity has lost its radiance when it has become primarily legalistic or dogmatic. It regains its radiance when it manifests a life of enthusiasm like that of the followers of Jesus concerning whom an anonymous writer of an early century said: "They are in the flesh, but they do not live after the flesh. They pass their days on earth, but they are the citizens of heaven. They obey the prescribed laws, and at the same time surpass the laws by their lives. . . . What the soul is in the body, that the Christians are in the world."[8]

CHAPTER EIGHT

The Ingredients of Happiness

THE RELIGION preached and exemplified by Jesus had happiness as an outstanding result. Eight successive statements in the fifth chapter of Matthew are known as the Beatitudes. Each begins with the word "blessed," *beati* in the Latin. The Greek word in the original New Testament was the ordinary word that people used when, for example, they wanted to congratulate someone. "You are a happy man!" they would say, using this word. The Aramaic, which Jesus employed, must have been the equivalent of the Hebrew that is in Psalm 1:1, "Blessed is the man." Professor James Moffatt translates that: "Happy is the man."

THE SEARCH FOR HAPPINESS

People want to be happy, but sometimes when they reach after happiness it eludes them. In 300 B.C. a philosopher named Epicurus was living in Athens. He noticed that people want to be happy. He observed that people naturally avoid pain and seek pleasure. He concluded, therefore, that lack of pleasure is the worst thing in life and that happiness is its chief good. His followers took up this idea very cheerfully, but as time went along they more and more vulgarized their master's teaching, until what we call popular Epicureanism came to have as its motto: "Let us eat, drink, and be merry, for tomorrow we die." Living in accordance with this philosophy, men attempted to seize pleasure wherever they got a glimpse of it, without regard for any other consideration whatsoever. The more they did this, the more that which they were trying to lay hold on seemed to slip through their fingers. The historians of the ancient world all describe this popular Epicureanism and at the same time comment upon the weariness with life which increasingly overcame the people who lived by that philosophy.

THE JOY OF JESUS

Jesus Christ, on the other hand, did not always do the thing that looked as if it would make for pleasure, but he did seem to have a deeper joy than most people. Many times he did things that appeared to be quite the opposite of what would bring pleasure. He did not seem to decide a matter primarily on whether it would make him happy to do the thing or not, but on quite other grounds. Therefore not a few times he did that which brought pain rather than pleasure. He did things which his best friends advised him not to do, and at last experienced cruel death at a youthful age. Nevertheless, as we read the gospels it is quite plain that Jesus experienced joy, that deep under the surface of his life was profound happiness.

It is therefore with a strong sense of listening to one who knows whereof he is speaking that we come to what Jesus says about happiness. When he uses the word customarily translated "blessed," it undoubtedly has a wide and rich meaning, but it certainly includes in part at least the idea of happiness. This is not something foreign to his religion but is an integral part of it. It will be proper to lay emphasis on this aspect of the matter in the present study of the Beatitudes by translating the word "blessed" each time as "happy."

HAPPY IS THE MAN

The first beatitude states, in the Revised Standard Version, "Blessed are the poor in spirit, for theirs is the kingdom of heaven."

Putting in our own words the part of the matter we are here concerned to study, we may read, "Happy is the humble man." Who is happy, he who is humble or he who is haughty? The opposite of humility is haughtiness. Is a haughty man happy? He cannot possibly be happy, because he has to worry all the time lest somebody is going to puncture the fine bubble of his inflated self. Jesus' mention of "the poor in spirit" may well have been a reference to the "people of the land," as they were called in that day. They were the opposite of the official classes. Among the official classes were the learned, but one of their own number had already said, "With more wisdom is more worry, and increase of knowledge is increase of sorrow."[1] Among the official classes were the rich people, and Jesus said that it was harder for one of them to get into the kingdom than for a camel to get through the eye of a needle. Among them were the powerful people. Power tends to corrupt. It corrupted a man like Herod Antipas quite completely. These people were not very happy. People who live complicated lives, full of intrigue, are not very happy. The ultimate evidence of unhappiness in life is doubtless suicide. Twenty-two thousand people a year in the United States end life this way. A study was made of the matter, and it was found that those who take this way out are commonly not people who are hard up against it, but rather those who have many advantages. One left this final word: "I have had few real difficulties; I have had, on the contrary, an exceptionally glamorous life as life goes, and I have had more than my share of affections and appreciations. . . . No one thing is responsible for this, and no one person—except myself."[2] Such persons are not as happy as those who live simply and humbly. So—

> *I would not be too wise—so very wise*
> *That I must sneer at simple songs and creeds,*
> *And let the glare of wisdom blind my eyes*
> *To humble people and their humble needs.*
>
> *I would not care to climb so high that I*
> *Could never hear the children at their play,*
> *Could only see the people passing by,*
> *And never hear the cheering words they say.*

I would not know too much—too much to smile
At trivial errors of the heart and hand,
Nor be too proud to play the friend the while,
Nor cease to help and know and understand.

I would not care to sit upon a throne,
Or build my house upon a mountain top,
Where I must dwell in glory all alone
And never friend come in or poor man stop.

God grant that I may live upon this earth,
And face the tasks which every morning brings,
And never lose the glory and the worth
Of humble service and the simple things.[3]

The second beatitude declares, "Blessed are those who mourn, for they shall be comforted." Happy, we may paraphrase, is the person who has a horizon of hope. Everyone will mourn, everyone will have sorrow. No one can build walls high enough to keep it out; no security provisions in any welfare state can ever ward it off. Who then can be happy? Only he who has a horizon that enables him to see out beyond. That was the trouble with the popular Epicureanism of the ancient world—it admitted no farther horizon. There was no necessity to live by any ultimate requirement, and when trouble came there was also nothing ultimate to hold onto or look unto. The futilitarian epitaphs of the ancient world already quoted are abundant evidence of this fact. They show how poorly prepared men were by that kind of philosophy to face the inescapable crisis of death. Happy is the person who sees something beyond. Happy is the man who shares in life's common experience of sorrow, not in utter hopelessness, but with a horizon to which he can look beyond sorrow.

Third, "Blessed are the meek, for they shall inherit the earth." Happy is the person who does not hurt somebody else to get what he is striving for. The opposite here is the dictator who rides roughshod over everybody else, and should be haunted to the end of his days by the faces of those he has trampled down. Happy is the person who does not hurt others. Lao Tzu, the ancient philosopher of China, compared this kind of life to water. "The highest good,"

he said, "is like that of water. The goodness of water is that it benefits the ten thousand creatures, yet itself does not scramble, but
is content with the places that all men disdain. It is this that makes
water so near to the Way. Nothing under heaven is softer or more
yielding than water; but when it attacks things hard and resistant,
there is not one of them that can prevail."

Fourth, "Blessed are those who hunger and thirst for righteousness, for they shall be satisfied." Happy is the man who looks to the
heights. Wherein does happiness lie? It lies in aspiration more than
in arrival; it lies in striving rather than in stagnation. Jawaharlal
Nehru has said, "The most significant period in my life was the
time when I was engaged in the struggle. Ultimately, perhaps the
only true joy for a person is to engage himself in some great cause,
in some elementary work, and to give all his strength and energy
to it." Happy is the man who is looking up at something and
striving for it.

Fifth, "Blessed are the merciful, for they shall obtain mercy."
Happy is the man who does not cherish hatred. When people do
things against us, there are just two possibilities—the possibility of
hatred and the possibility of mercy. The trouble with hatred is that
it harms ourselves even more than the other person. If we respond
by hate we may concoct or devise some method of inflicting punishment upon the other person. Almost inevitably we will suffer a
deeper punishment within ourselves and we will never be happy.
A friend said to E. Stanley Jones: "Resentments have divided our
family. I have two brothers and two sisters. I am the only one who
is friendly with all the others. Some of these resentments are twenty-
five years old. . . . Love is the only way to keep a family together."
Think of spoiling twenty-five years with resentment! Happy is no
man who does that. Howard Thurman has said, "If we nourish
within our hearts hate and fear and self-centeredness, we shall
spend our days stumbling in the dark." Margaret Evelyn Singleton
has written:

> *I fear no hell in afterlife*
> *As torturous as my own*
> *That lacerates the tender flesh*
> *When Hate ascends the throne.*

The dark descent to Hades' heart
Reluctant and alone
I make, and learn the mockery
Of life when love has flown.[4]

Happy is the man who does not cherish hate.

Sixth, "Blessed are the pure in heart, for they shall see God."
Happy is the man who has a healthy conscience. There are two
things that can go wrong with conscience. One is that you will not
pay any attention to it, that you will dull it, that you will push back
its gentle intimations to you and so land in some morass of evil,
and in that there is no happiness. The other thing that can go
wrong with conscience is that you will whip it up and stimulate
it to such an over-sensitivity that it becomes a morbid thing and
turns all of life into unhappiness. Happy is the person who has a
healthy conscience that is a dependable guide through the perplex-
ing alternatives that confront us as we walk in life.

Seventh, "Blessed are the peacemakers, for they shall be called
sons of God." Happy are the people who heal divisions in the
world. We can appropriately make our prayer with St. Francis of
Assisi:

> Lord, make me an instrument of your peace; where there is
> hatred, let me sow love; where there is injury, pardon; where there
> is doubt, faith; where there is despair, hope; where there is dark-
> ness, light; and where there is sadness, joy.

Eighth, "Blessed are those who are persecuted for righteousness'
sake, for theirs is the kingdom of heaven." Happy is the heroic man
who does what is hard and right, even if he suffers for it. The
Epicurean idea was to do what was easy, and doing what was easy,
people came often to frustration and futility. Doing what is hard,
people have many times afterward come to experience a glowing
sense of happiness. Persecution was grimly real to the early Christians. Those who have studied the lives of the martyrs among the
early Christians have found that they really experienced joy. They
sometimes had such joy that it made them oblivious to the torments
which men inflicted on them. In the tremendous climax of Sholem
Asch's *The Apostle*, he describes the Christian martyrs under Nero.

They were lifted up by a sublime joy that made them able for the utmost that they had to experience. In our day, the persecution is apt to be more subtle and perhaps as difficult to endure, but let us try to do the hard thing, for with the doing of what is hard comes happiness.

Here then are eight statements from the gospel of Jesus. They run counter to much popular thought, but back of them is the life of Jesus Christ who had deep joy despite much trouble. Back of them is the happiest life, as far as we know, in spite of pain and sorrow, the world has ever seen. It would therefore be worth trying, instead of reaching out and attempting to seize something that is immediately pleasurable, without regard to any other consideration, to take one or many of these ways. Then having for the moment forgotten all about the pursuit of happiness, we may find that it will come and make its abiding presence with us forevermore.

CHAPTER NINE

If Thine Eye Be Single

THE PROFOUND insight of Jesus into the nature of man and the way of life is evident throughout his teaching. Often these teachings are concentrated into a single sentence, and it may be not only so compact but also so picturesquely phrased as to be momentarily puzzling. The statement recorded in Matthew 6:22 is a very good example. "If," said Jesus, "thine eye be single, thy whole body shall be full of light."

What does it mean to have an eye that is single? Interpreters have offered varying translations of the word "single" in order to bring out different aspects of its possible significance. Edgar J. Goodspeed has suggested that the word really means "sound," and has been followed in this by the Revised Standard Version which reads: "If your eye is sound, your whole body will be full of light." James Moffatt has translated "generous": "If your Eye is generous, the whole of your body will be illumined." In the original Greek, however, the word plainly means "single" or "onefold" as over against another Greek word which means "double" or "twofold." Therefore the statement of Jesus must mean to have one's eye fixed upon one definite object. To have an eye that is single is a symbolic expression for singleness of purpose.

Of course, it is sometimes helpful to be able to look in different directions and to think different thoughts at the same time. A fly has many facets in its eye and can see in many different directions at once. That is why it escapes destruction as often as it does. A pedestrian in our day has to be able to look in both directions at once, to survive very long. A teacher is reputed to have eyes in the back of her head, and most young people doubtless think that is a prerequisite for entering the profession. For their part, young people now seem to have to be able to study their English, Spanish, and Algebra and look at television at the same time. Nevertheless, with some such reasonable exceptions as these, we are led by the statement of Jesus to consider the importance of singleness of purpose; of looking at one great object; of having an eye that is single.

IF THINE EYE BE NOT SINGLE

It is clear that failure to have an eye that is single is the source of frustration, ineffectiveness, and unhappiness in some lives. The person who does not have an eye that is single may be disorganized. All of us doubtless start out in life unorganized. Henry Hitt Crane once described a baby which he saw on the train. It was not very well co-ordinated yet. It was trying to put its thumb in its mouth, but got only as close as getting it into its ear. We all start out relatively unorganized, but if later in life we remain in that state it is unfortunate. Stephen Leacock, the humorist, created an unforgettable figure when he described the horseman who flung himself upon his horse and rode madly off in all directions. That is a poor way to get to any single goal. Queen Victoria used to complain that her Prime Minister, Gladstone, talked to her as if he were addressing a public meeting. Ralph W. Sockman says that we all, in a sense, are public meetings, with many parts of our nature moving resolutions and many desires clamoring for a vote. One writer says of a character in a novel: "He was not so much a human being as a civil war." And one modern person has said, "I would know myself better if there were not so many of me." Even so, a person came to Jesus for help a long time ago and said, "My name is Legion; for we are many."[1] If we are disorganized we are probably experiencing frustration in life.

Again, the person who does not have an eye that is single is a person who may be divided against himself, and thus be ineffective. I am told that in Chinese the symbol for the personal pronoun "I" is a set of crossed swords. That is "I" to some of us, indeed. Some of us are in conflict because there is a difference between our work and our wishes. Some people are chained to a desk, and wish they could be traveling in the far places of the earth. Some men are employed as traveling salesmen, and wish nothing so much as to be at home working in the garden. Some are engineers, and wish they had the courage to go into the ministry. Some are ministers, and wish they could peacefully plow corn. Some of us have conflict between our minds and our hearts. In our hearts we are devoted to our childhood faith. But our minds have been educated in a modern university and introduced to far frontiers of philosophy and thought. We have never gotten the two together, our faith and our philosophy. Worst of all, in some of our lives there is perhaps an unreconciled conflict going on between our better nature and our worse nature. Our higher nature and our lower nature war with each other, and a person is miserably unhappy in the midst of such conflict. There are at least two classical statements in literature on this conflict. One is by the apostle Paul in the seventh chapter of his letter to the Romans: "I do not do the good I want, but the evil I do not want is what I do. . . . I delight in the law of God, in my inmost self, but I see in my members another law at war with the law of my mind. . . . Wretched man that I am!" The other is by Augustine in his *Confessions:* "And thus there are two wills and neither is entire. I neither willed entirely, nor yet was I entirely unwilling; therefore was I at war with myself and divided against myself. One and the same soul it is, but with half itself willeth this and with its other half willeth that. . . . So these two wills, one old, one new, one carnal, one spiritual, contended with each other and disturbed my soul."

There is yet another way in which we may fail to have a single eye, and this is if we ever live in duplicity. The Greek word which is the opposite of the word in our text means double or twofold, and in Latin is *duplex.* This we carry over into English, and then in English derive from it the further word "duplicity." That means doubleness of heart or speech; deception by pretending to entertain one set of feelings and acting under the influence of another; bad faith; double dealing.

In this connection, two characters in *Pilgrim's Progress* by that great master of characterization, John Bunyan, come to mind. One of them was Mr. Facing Both Ways. The other was Mr. By-ends, "whose ancestor was a waterman, looking one way and rowing the other." Jesus was more severe when he talked about this kind of people than almost any other. He seemed to have pity for people who were involved in gross sins. They were probably suffering enough, or going to, soon. But about people who were living in conscious hypocrisy, professedly one thing and privately another, he spoke very severely. Of the scribes and Pharisees he said that insofar as they were setting forth the law of Moses, men should do what they said, but that men should not do what they did, for they preached and did not practice. Now if we are living in any of these states of disorganization, or division against ourselves, or duplicity, it is quite plain that we do not have this eye that is single, and it is understandable that we experience darkness in our lives instead of light. Jesus said elsewhere that a house or kingdom divided against itself cannot stand. And James remarked that a double-minded man is unstable in all his ways.[2]

IF THINE EYE BE INDEED SINGLE

Positively, then, in the saying of Jesus is suggested the secret of satisfaction, effectiveness, and happiness in life. "If thine eye be single, thy whole body shall be full of light." Consider what a satisfaction it is to have a sense of direction. Sometimes it seems to take something outside of us to give us this sense. In World War II an eighteen-year-old young man, Jay Topkis, wrote in the *New York Times*: "My whole life has shifted focus. . . . It's ironic, but it's taken a war to give me an objective, and I think that is true of most of the fellows around my age. I, frankly, have been floundering; I haven't known how to aim my life. Sometimes I have thought I am a writer, and I am registered in college as pre-law. My thoughts, hopes and judgment of my capacities move about like pieces in a kaleidoscope. But there is one hard, solid, central piece that does not change, and this is the fact that I am enlisted in the army reserve."

It is better, however, if the world permits and if there is something within us that rises up to produce a sense of direction. A mother came to Edgar DeWitt Jones because she was concerned about her son. She said that he was more interested in snakes than in anything else. He studied snakes, handled them, read everything he could find about them. Dr. Jones asked the mother to have the son come to see him. This she promised, and he came. Dr. Jones liked his looks, for he was clear-eyed, sturdy, of good appearance. He asked him what he expected to do in life. The lad answered, "I want to be a herpetologist." The boy wanted to know all that was to be known about the snakes of the world. When he talked about it his eyes flashed, his face shone. He was really interested. Dr. Jones, wisely, wrote to the mother to let the boy follow his bent, for some day she might be the mother of a worthy successor to the late Dr. Ditmars, who was the leading herpetologist of his day.

To have an eye that is single means also to find deliverance from division within us. There is a great joy in finding that deliverance. It may be in finding the work that we ought to be doing, and going into it, even at a sacrifice. It may be in a long process of getting our heart and mind together, so that our faith and our philosophy are congruous one with the other; so, as Tennyson put it,

> *That mind and soul, according well*
> *May make one music as before,*
> *But vaster.*

Above all, there is a great joy in coming to deliverance out of that inner conflict between the better and the worse within us. That conflict can be very terrible. Into the Personal Trouble Clinic of a certain church a man came one day with haggard face and a wild look in his eyes. He begged for help to find a way out from an existence, every moment of which had become torture to him. He was suffering from mental delusions; his mind had no rest by day or night. He thought that he was being pursued by strange creatures, and in his fantasy he was terribly tormented. The counselor finally pieced together the facts of his story. He had spent his early life in an idealistic environment, in which he had built up lofty standards of moral conduct. Then he had come to a great city and had fallen into one vice after another. Finally he found himself at the center of a moral conflict that was terrific in intensity. Ultimately he became the victim of these delusions of the mind. A process of re-education and of reconditioning to the good had to be undertaken. It was slow; it took months to bring him to peace again, out of that storm-driven experience. Part of the therapy that was needed to lift him up was a continuous prayer life and a constant affirmation of spiritual power. At last he came up out of the terrible division into which he had fallen, and found peace.[3]

To have an eye that is single is also to have the effectiveness in life that a man has who straightforwardly, steadfastly does his duty. Hazen G. Werner, who narrates the incident summarized in the preceding paragraph in his book *And We Are Whole Again,* there calls attention also to the priest in Willa Cather's *Shadows on the Rock.* He is a man who gave up culture and intellectual pursuits in France to minister in a primitive area of eastern Canada. There may be a chance to return home, but Father Hector refuses it with these words:

Thank you, but no. I have taken a vow that will spoil your plans for me. I shall not return to France. . . . Listen, my friend. No man can give himself heart and soul to one thing while in the back of his mind he cherishes a desire, a secret hope, for something very different. You, as a student, must know that even in worldly affairs nothing worth while is accomplished except by that last sacrifice, the giving of oneself altogether and finally. Since I made that final sacrifice, I have been twice the man I was before.[4]

Therefore, to have an eye that is single must mean at least these things. Indeed, when these things come about in life—that we find a sense of direction, get deliverance from conflicting tensions, and find a duty in the line of which we can walk steadily forward—then we live in light instead of darkness. As the psychologist Dr. William H. Sheldon says, "Happiness is essentially a state of going somewhere, wholeheartedly, one-directionally, without regret or reservation."

THE WAY OF DISCIPLESHIP

Finally, we may note that the very best way to come to have the eye that is single is to set out to follow Jesus. Who is it that says this word which so immediately sheds a flood of light upon life and its problems? Even Jesus! He seems to understand our hearts better than we ourselves, and again and again his word in a concentrated way says the thing that is the clue to our difficulty and the way out of it. What is the goal that is great enough to command every person's ultimate loyalty? The kingdom of God, for which Jesus lived and died, and which he compared to a treasure hidden in a field, so precious that it is worth while to sell everything else in order to obtain it.[5] Who is of such spotless character and such kindly yet commanding presence as to deserve our utmost personal devotion and loyalty? Jesus Christ! And in discipleship to him a multitude of people have found the way to rise above the dangers of disorganization and division and duplicity into this directional living, this delivered living, this dutiful living, in which there is light indeed.

CHAPTER TEN

When He Came to Himself

J ESUS' penetrating understanding of life is manifest not only in his aphorisms but also in his parables. Of these matchlessly lucid stories, that concerning the prodigal son is perhaps the best known of all. This parable is usually studied as a matter of the relationship between the son and his father, or as a matter of the relationship between the son and his older brother, who remained at home while he went away. The turning point in the story is reached, however, with the words which are found in Luke 15:17, "But when he came to himself," and they suggest that the narrative may also be studied in terms of the relationship between the prodigal son and himself.

STAGES IN THE RELATIONSHIP

Several successive stages are clearly observable in this relationship. At first the prodigal son was at war with himself. This was when he was still at home and was trying to make up his mind whether or not to go away. He was struggling with himself over that question. In common with all young people, his thoughts were long, long thoughts; he felt great powers stirring within himself. Like many a young person he felt under restrictions at home. And like all people, he was a battlefield for the impulses of both good and evil. Robert Browning has described man at such a point of struggle:

> *God stoops o'er his head,*
> *Satan looks up between his feet—both tug—*
> *He's left, himself, i' the middle.*

The next stage was when the prodigal son was not himself. We can imagine that as he went off down the long road, his father looked sadly after him and shook his head and said, "He is not himself today." He had hardly been himself for quite a while, and now he certainly was different from his former self. He was no longer the boy who had grown up at home and taken delight in many wonderful, worth-while things. He was a different person as he went on the long road away.

The next stage in his experience found him outside himself. Now he is in a far country. In this far country he abandons himself to riotous living; without restraint and without hesitation he plunges into all the excesses that attract him, paying out his money freely for such purposes. At this point he thinks that everything is thrilling and exciting. He is in a veritable ecstasy of uninhibited behavior. But the word ecstasy has an interesting etymology. It is made up of two Greek words which mean "out of" and "standing," and he was standing outside of himself at this time. He was in a transport of abandon that carried him quite outside himself.

At the next point he came to be beside himself. The consequences of what he had done began to catch up with him. E. Stanley Jones remarks that everybody gets either results or consequences. You get results that you work for ahead of time; you get consequences that follow inevitably from what you have done. So the consequences of his behavior overtake him. As this happens, he becomes increasingly desperate. He has exhausted all his money, and those who helped him spend it have disappeared. Those who assisted him at each step on the downward path are now laughing at him for having struck the bottom of it. He has indeed reached the bottom. He was from a Jewish home, and now he must feed swine, quite the lowest and most humiliating occupation thinkable from his background. Amidst the famine which was ravaging the country, he even wished that he could eat the husks on which the swine were fed. In this state of desperation he is beside himself with fear and dread of what is going to happen to him. More than

one young person has plunged gaily into sin, thinking that he
would not be afraid of anything, that he was in no wise a coward,
only to find that from the very beginning of his entrance upon the
pathway of sin, fear follows him and haunts him. For the first
time in his life he is really afraid, and he will never cease being
afraid until he ceases walking upon that pathway. In the words of
Coleridge, he is

> *Like one that on a lonesome road*
> *Doth walk in fear and dread,*
> *And having once turned round, walks on*
> *And turns no more his head;*
> *Because he knows a frightful fiend*
> *Doth close behind him tread.*

Next, the prodigal son became ashamed of himself, and here his
healing and recovery began. At last he realizes that this is not, after
all, what he had meant to do with his life. This does not correspond to his real desire and his deep purpose. He begins to be
aware that he has actually done wrong. His experience is like that
described by Harry Emerson Fosdick:

> We have done something really wrong—violated a trust, be-
> trayed a friend, outraged inner standards of conduct whose validity
> we can no more deny than a scientist can deny his duty to be hon-
> est with his facts. We discover that when we have accepted a
> code of the utmost moral latitude and have added to this ethical
> liberality all the alibis and rationalizations we can lay our minds to,
> there still are standards of right conduct not to be escaped. No lati-
> tudinarian interpretations can make Judas Iscariot right, any more
> than they can make it right for a scientist to fudge his sums or for
> an artist to do deliberately shoddy work. Some behavior is really
> wrong.[1]

The prodigal son has come up against this hard fact. With shame
he must ask himself, in the words of the poet, Clarence Edwin
Flynn:

> *To be a slave when one might be a king,*
> *To walk low roads when one might tread the high,*

To crawl when one might just as well take wing,
To take the slime when one might have the sky,
To company with those whose lives are cheap
When with the sons of God one might commune,
To have the shallow rather than the deep,
To choose the discord rather than the tune,
To dwell in swamps when one might brave the height,
To have a hovel for the heart and miss
The golden dome where it might dwell in light—
Is there a greater tragedy than this?

The next stage in the spiritual pilgrimage of the prodigal son is that indicated by the words, "When he came to himself." At this point he feels as if he has been away from himself for a long time and is just getting back. He feels as if he has been in a terrible illness and is just beginning to convalesce and come out of it. And thus it was that at last the prodigal son came to himself.

FOUR TRUTHS

Implicit in this story are at least four great truths. The first is that a person cannot run away from himself. The son ran away from home and got very quickly out of the range of his father's voice. Had his father called after him, he would have soon been too far to hear that familiar voice. He not only soon got beyond the family farm limits, he even left his home country behind. Going perhaps to one of the Hellenistic cities in Transjordan or even farther away than that, he was no longer in the Jewish land and subject to the Jewish rules and regulations that had hemmed him in and restricted him so badly. He got away from everything except himself. There is a story about Ralph Waldo Emerson, who once went to Italy to get away from himself, but when he got there, there was Ralph Waldo Emerson! Passengers on an excursion liner at sea were asked why they were taking the voyage. A surprisingly large percentage of them replied that they were doing it in the hope of forgetting themselves. But I am sure that each one still had himself right there on his hands. One cannot run away from one's self.

The second truth is that integrity is a priceless possession. "When we cultivate integrity," John Erskine said, "we begin by dreaming of a world within us which shall have all the rest of life as attendant and servant." Plato said, "The first and best victory is to conquer self; to be conquered by self is, of all things, the most shameful and vile." In the play, *Cyrano de Bergerac,* defeated and yet undefeated, Cyrano speaks these words at the end:

> *One thing without stain,*
> *Unspotted from the world, in spite of doom*
> *Mine own!—*
> *And that is . . .*
> *My white plume!*

We salute those who have kept unstained from the world their white plume, have kept it high. Personal integrity, unstained and uncompromised, is a great and priceless possession. Hold it precious and priceless.

The third truth is that man is fundamentally good. In classical Chinese philosophy, three philosophers engaged in a discussion of the nature of man. Hsün Tzu thought that man was inherently and essentially bad, and said: "The nature of man is evil; his goodness is only acquired training." Kao Tzu held that man cannot tell the difference between good and evil. He put it in this simile: "Our nature is like a whirlpool: if a breach is made to the east, the water flows east; if a breach is made to the west, it flows west. As water does not discern between east and west, so man's nature does not discern between good and evil." Meng Tzu, whom we know better as Mencius, a disciple of the great Confucius, advanced a third position. Answering the argument of Kao Tzu, he said: "Truly water does not discern between east and west, but does it not discern between up and down? Man's nature is good, as water flows down. No man but is good, no water but flows down. Hit water and make it leap, you can send it above your forehead; force it, and you can bring it up a hill. But is that the nature of water? It is done by force; and when man is brought to do evil, the same is done to his nature."

It would appear that the parable of the prodigal son assumes that man has deep at the center of his life something fundamentally good. His evil is a departure from that which is deepest within himself; his repentance is a returning to that same center of his being. No doubt any such thing was hard to realize, when the prodigal son was seen in the depths of his degradation. There he was, dissolute, disheveled, dejected, a pitiable sight. Yet even then deep inside himself there was still something good, and he was still capable of coming back to himself. Therefore, in even the lowliest prisoner in solitary confinement on Alcatraz there must still be something that is good, at the center of his life. If he could only get back to it before it is too late!

The fourth truth lies in the fact that if we are ourselves, then we know that we belong to God and that we belong with God. This story is transparently intended to reveal the relationships of God and man. The father is at last none other than the heavenly Father, and the son is any man who wanders away from him. When he comes back to himself, then he knows that he belongs to God, and that he belongs with God. When the prodigal son came to himself, he said, "I will arise and go to my father." Augustine said in classical words: "Thou hast made us for Thyself, and our hearts are restless until they find rest in Thee."

WHAT BRINGS ONE BACK TO ONESELF?

What is it that brings a man back to himself? Disaster does it sometimes. In the case of the prodigal son, it was famine. The outward catastrophe was an instrument in his redemption. As in the case of the prodigal son, it is sometimes not until we have walked along a road far enough to come into calamity that we are brought to our senses. If disaster halts us upon a road of sin and brings us back to ourselves, we shall be grateful, I think, for its ministration.

Remembrance was another thing that helped bring the prodigal son to himself. All the time he never altogether forgot home and father and the happiness that was there. Yet another factor was love—the love of his father. That was a real force, an actual power reaching across those many miles and exerting its pull upon him all the time. Professor J. B. Rhine speaks about "the reach of the mind," and demonstrates that it has an outreaching power beyond what we usually think. The father's love was really reaching across those many miles and exercising an attractive force upon that son to bring him back home. Even so, assuredly the love of God is a real power, an actual force, just as actual as the power of gravitation, reaching out to wherever we are and exerting its attractive power to draw us unto himself. There is nothing God wants so much as that we should say, if we have ever gone far away like the prodigal son and then like him have come to ourselves again, "I will arise and go to my father."

CHAPTER ELEVEN

The Reticence of Christ

INCISIVE and authoritative as was the aphoristic and parabolical utterance of Jesus, there were many occasions when he said less than was expected, or nothing at all. This was contrary to popular expectation relative to the Messiah. "I know that Messiah is coming (he who is called Christ)," said the Samaritan woman according to John 4:25; "when he comes, he will show us all things." Modern followers of Christ, too, may readily assume that he will answer all questions, solve all problems, and reveal all things. But when men came to him then, and when we come to him now, they encountered and we find a reticence which may seem strange.

Reticence means saying less than is expected. It means restraint in speech, and keeping quiet. It is the opposite of talkativeness, garrulousness, forwardness, and self-assertiveness. In Christ there is what Tennyson calls "a fine reserve and a noble reticence." Here are several examples of it.

One we find in the case of his relationship to the man who wanted him to solve his personal problems. Jesus was in the midst of a multitude. A man out of the multitude called to him and said, "Teacher, bid my brother divide the inheritance with me."[1] We can reconstruct the situation. Here is a man who has come into a dispute with his own brother over the property that has come down from the deceased parents. He is perhaps involved in litigation and an outright lawsuit over the heritage. Now Jesus, the great teacher, is present. The man will get him to decide the matter, preferably of course on his own side. It might seem as if this were an important opportunity for Jesus to speak, to utter a decisive word. Did not Moses decide disputes among his people? Was not Solomon famous for his classic decision when the two women disputed over the one child? Was this not an occasion on which Jesus might properly utter a decision which would clarify the disputed matter and at the same time establish himself as an authority? Instead, we find that he declines to speak on the subject. He replies to the man simply, "Man, who made me a judge or divider over you?" Then he did go on and tell a story—a story about a rich fool—which, if this man had ears to hear, was a clue as to what was wrong within his own life and why he was so frequently becoming involved in such matters. But Jesus did not settle the man's dispute for him. He left that up to the man.

Another example of the reticence of Christ is in the case where outright condemnation of a sinner was expected. Scribes and Pharisees, who were the exemplars and guardians of righteousness, brought before him a woman taken in adultery. "Moses commanded us to stone such," they said. "What do you say about her?" Again what an evident opportunity, what an apparent opening for Jesus to say a word that would cause all sinners everywhere to cringe and tremble! But he did not say a single word this time. The reticent Christ stooped over and wrote on the ground. The scribes and Pharisees continued to press him to say something, and so he rose up and said, "Let him who is without sin among you be the first to throw a stone at her." Then he stooped over and wrote on the ground again. They began to go away, beginning with the eldest. Then he looked at the woman and asked, "Has no one condemned you?" She said, "No one, Lord." Then Jesus Christ said, "Neither do I condemn you; go, and do not sin again."[2]

Again we recall the reticence of Christ in connection with the inquiry about when the end of the world would take place. He had told the disciples that Jerusalem would be destroyed and the Temple be razed to the ground, and he had intimated that the end of the world would come and the last Judgment of God take place.

With the natural curiosity that all of us have, the disciples asked, "When will this be?" What an opportunity it was to say a word! Who would not desire to enhance his prophetic prestige by making a prognostication that would come true? But Jesus said: "No one knows, not even the angels in heaven, nor the Son, but only the Father."[3]

Once more the reticence of Christ comes before us in the matter of who he himself was. That question was asked by many people. Perhaps the most dramatic incident was when Jesus stood as a prisoner before Pilate. Pilate asked the question, "Are you the King of the Jews?" Here was an occasion when Jesus might make an unequivocal answer, might set forth his divine dignity in unmistakable words against the backdrop of that Roman court, whence it would surely echo throughout the Roman Empire. But the reticent Christ simply replied to Pilate, "You have said so."[4]

There are three conclusions which we may draw from the reticence of Christ.

WARNING

The first one is in the nature of warning. We who are followers of Christ and a part of his church ought not to be more forward and more self-assertive than Jesus himself was. Sometimes we are tempted to be. We are tempted as Christians and as a church to try to settle affairs which we are not competent to settle. Once upon a time the church attempted to do that in relation to science. The church tried to tell science what was true, without itself taking the trouble to find out in the hard painstaking way, as science was doing. The church undertook to rebuke Copernicus and Galileo and their fellows for their astronomical investigations, and Darwin for his biological studies. It would have behooved the church to be more reticent. In our day, we undertake to tell the nations how to handle international affairs. By all means we should try to bring the spirit and teaching of Christ to bear upon the affairs of the nations. Perhaps, however, we ought to do it with a little more humility and even reticence than sometimes we have done. In a joint assembly of various denominations, many addresses were devoted to admonishing and exhorting the nations to unite. One observer in that gathering remarked that it was a rather strange spectacle to see the churches telling the nations to get together, when they themselves were not together, when they were still so terribly divided. It might be well if we worked as hard as we could first of all to bring the churches together, and then, with that experience by way of authority, continued to try to lead the nations to unite.

Again, when as Christians we try to tell other people how to live their lives and manage their affairs, we may be going beyond the bounds that are suggested by the reticence of Christ. Also we are going too far when we utter harsh and hasty judgments upon other people. I wonder where we would have been in that scene that day when the scribes and Pharisees were so ready to condemn and Christ was so slow to condemn? With whom would we instinctively have agreed?

Likewise we are tempted to go beyond the bounds of the reticence of Christ in the very matter of calculating when the end of the world will come. Christians down through all the centuries have forgotten that Jesus did not know and would not say, and they have tried to find out and declare the answer. In A.D. 500 it was thought the end of the world was due that year, and in A.D. 1000 it was thought so again. Later the date of 1260 was established, then the dates of 1365, 1533, 1914, 1930, 1934, and so on down. We would do well to remember that Jesus said, "No one knows."

Furthermore, when we try to compress the boundless greatness of Christ within the limits of a tiny formula, we would do well to remember this same thing. There was a famous council of the church once upon a time which tried to do that. There were two parties within the council. The one had a word that was spelled with a diphthong, and they believed that it expressed the truth. The other had a word that was spelled with a single vowel instead, and they believed that word embodied the correct doctrine. They excommunicated each other, anathematized each other, and each was sure that it had the boundless greatness of Christ within its own little word! On all of these points we would do well to take warning from the restraint and the reticence of Jesus himself.

ENCOURAGEMENT

The second conclusion is in the nature of encouragement. I find it definitely encouraging that Jesus was reticent on so many of these things. I derive from this fact the encouraging belief that it is not necessary to understand everything in order to be a Christian. Jesus Christ himself did not answer all questions, and tell all things to his disciples. There are some people who are staying out of the church and out of the Christian life because they do not understand all of it. Do not stay out on that account. Who does understand all of it? Jesus himself did not undertake to explain everything to men. Almost everybody has some areas of doubt, some matters of uncertainty within his mind. Do not let that keep you out of active Christian fellowship and faith. Almost everyone also has something he believes. When he comes over against Christ he experiences a desire to respond to his call. Go ahead and do it without waiting until you have gotten an answer to all questions. Jesus does not expect complete knowledge; he wants us to have faith.

The reticence of Christ also encourages us to believe that the minister does not have to solve all problems as he proclaims the Christian gospel. It is extremely difficult if a minister has to be an authority in economics and international affairs and politics and all kinds of societal organization—but he does not. Jesus did not give a blueprint and make an authoritative pronouncement on each one of these matters. Albert Schweitzer says, "Beware of preaching the gospel as if it explained everything."

Again, it is encouraging to know that Christians may have honest differences of opinion. If Jesus had given us an absolute blueprint for everything and had told us the final answer on everything, then we would all have to believe absolutely alike. But he did not. He was reticent about such matters. That means we have an opportunity for honest difference of opinion, and we can still be a part of his fellowship and still be Christians. That is true relative to economics, to politics, and even to theology.

CHALLENGE

The third conclusion is in the nature of challenge. The reticence of Christ constitutes his greatest challenge to us. It means that he is leaving part of the matter up to us. This man wants Christ to settle his personal affairs. Instead of that, Jesus tells a story, and if the man will he can secure the clue to settle that personal affair and the rest of the affairs of his life in the light of it. Jesus expects him to do his part. He challenges him, as it were, by his very unwillingness to step in and give the answer, ready made. As for the woman, there is yet something within her that is fine enough to guide her, and Jesus wants that to have a chance to speak. The disciples would like to know about the future course of the world; instead they are to live by faith from day to day. As for the matter of their belief in him, he is not even going to force that upon them.

Therefore, we are challenged by the reticence of Christ. In our personal affairs, he gives us the clue, the great principle, and then leaves it to us to apply it in the detailed ramifications of living. As we wonder where the world is going, we do not find that he tells us all about it ahead of time. He challenges us to live by faith and to walk by faith. And in our answer to Jesus himself, he leaves part of it up to us. Once the question came up as to whether, if a person should return from the dead, that would persuade people to believe. Jesus said, "If they do not hear Moses and the prophets, neither will they be convinced if some one should rise from the dead."[5] There is no outward spectacular event which can force belief. Jesus Christ does not compel. He stands before men in his matchless splendor, in the glory of his life, until something in us responds to that which we see before us. He forces nothing upon us; he watches and waits to see what we are going to do, how we are going to solve the problem, live, walk by faith, respond to him. The reticence of Christ is the very challenge of Christ.

CHAPTER TWELVE

When the Lamp Smolders

JESUS WAS not only reticent, thus showing that he respected the persons with whom he dealt; he was also gentle, thus showing that he desired to encourage them. One of the most striking statements of this fact is to be found in the quotation relative to his work of the prophecy of Isaiah: "A bruised reed shall he not break, and smoking flax shall he not quench."[1]

The oil lamp was the method of illumination in the Biblical world for thousands of years. In the museum of the Palestine Institute of Archaeology at Pacific School of Religion there is a display case containing lamps from the ancient world. The accompanying placard reads: "Light during 4000 years." It explains how ancient man was afraid of the dark because he thought of it as a place of evil and of danger. For him, light was not only a convenience which extended the day; it was also a means of keeping the powers of darkness at a distance, and a source of safety and solace. In the case are lamps which men made and used over a period of four thousand years. The earliest ones are dated in the fourth millennium B.C., that is between 4000 and 3000 B.C. These lamps are simply small pottery bowls. Olive oil was put in the bowl. A wick was made out of flax, by a process that can be duplicated today. The wick was dipped into the olive oil and laid over the edge of the bowl. It was lighted, and there it burned. On the edge of these bowls from three or four thousands years B.C. you can still see the soot marks where the wick burned. In the case of a lamp which was used a great deal, with the wick laid around at different places on the edge, the entire rim of the bowl may be black. By about 2000 B.C. an improvement was made in these lamps. As the potter made the clay bowl, he pinched the edge together at one spot to make a sort of groove or channel in which the wick could lie. Later a further improvement was made by folding the edges of that little channel over toward each other. By the time of the Greeks and Romans the lamps were molded with a cover over them and a round opening to put in the oil and what was practically a spout to hold the wick. This is the kind of lamp which was in use in New Testament days. In early Christian times even more elaborate examples were made. One is a large ring or circle with eleven spouts coming out all around. It was hung in one of the catacombs at Rome.

The basic principle involved in these lamps was of course the same that was in use up until within our own lifetime. All of us who ever lived in remote places where there was no electricity probably used lamps which, even if they were made of glass and metal and employed a different fluid and a different kind of wick, nevertheless produced light by the same fundamental principle. Indeed, that was the basic principle of illumination for the whole world until October 21, 1879, when Thomas A. Edison succeeded for the first time, after spending forty thousand dollars in fruitless experiments, in producing an incandescent lamp. Then in his laboratory a filament of carbonized cotton thread with electricity passing through it glowed in a vacuum for forty hours—the first incandescent lamp in history. From that time on we have enjoyed the brilliance of modern illumination. But until then the little oil lamp was the method of illumination.

This enables us to understand the otherwise somewhat enigmatical text quoted above, "and smoking flax shall he not quench." The flax is the wick dipped in the olive oil and laid over the edge of the little pottery lamp of long ago. Something has happened now. The oil has run low, the wick become clogged, or a draft of wind has almost blown out the flame. The wick is smoldering. Only a bit of spark is left in it. But Jesus will not put it out. In such a moment as this we can touch that wick with a finger and snuff it out almost instantly. Or with patient care, we may possibly nurse it back to life again. The latter is what he will do. Thus are explained the different translations of the verse. It was quoted above as it stands in the Authorized or King James Version, and it is translated similarly in the American Standard Version. If, however, you read the new translation of the Revised Standard Version it is like this: "He will not break a bruised reed or quench a smoldering wick." The smoking flax is the smoldering wick. Goodspeed's translation is: "He will not break off a bent reed, and he will not put out a smoldering wick." Moffatt retains the word "flax": "He will not break the bruised reed, he will not put out the smouldering flax."

This statement occurs originally in the Old Testament in the forty-second chapter of Isaiah, where it has to do with the Servant of the Lord. In quoting the passage, Matthew applies it to Jesus Christ and identifies him as the Servant of the Lord. When there was a man in the synagogue whose hand was withered, Jesus was kind to him. When Christ did his work, he did it with gentle concern for everybody. If there was even a spark of the spirit left, he would not snuff it out. He would not put out the smoldering wick, the smoking flax. He would help—it was said of Jesus Christ.

THE SMOKING WICK

There are many times in life when the lamp flickers, but Jesus Christ will not put it out. The flickering lamp? It is for one thing our finite knowledge. All of man's knowledge is really only a smoky flame in the midst of a great darkness. As Santayana puts it:

> *Our knowledge is a torch of smoky pine*
> *That lights the pathway but one step ahead*
> *Across a void of mystery and dread.*

Sometimes the darkness crowds in, some dark happening takes place, and the mind reels before it. We cannot understand why this terrible thing must be. Indeed, our knowledge is finite and limited. But Christ does not despise our minds. He encourages us as far as possible to think and understand, and to push back the darkness of superstition and of ignorance. In every far foreign land to which I have gone there have been schools established by missionaries and carried on by Christians in that land, because they believe, under the influence of Christ, that such work is important and that people should be helped to conquer ignorance and super- stition. Authentic Christianity believes that man's knowledge should be increased as much as possible.

The flickering lamp is also our feeble faith. Some of us may feel like the man in the New Testament who came to Jesus and said, "I believe; help my unbelief."[2] Some of us may feel like the men who voyaged with Jesus across the Sea of Galilee. At first all was calm, then the sudden storm came, and in their terror and anxiety they cried to him, "Master, we perish."[3] He, awaking from his sleep, told them to be quiet and spoke of them as men of little faith. In the storms of life, all of us are sometimes of little faith. But Christ never puts out the tiniest spark of faith in anybody's life. He helps it to increase. This we need, for where our knowledge reaches its limit, only faith can lead. With Santayana again we say:

> *Bid, then, the tender light of faith to shine*
> *By which alone the mortal heart is led*
> *Unto the thinking of the thought divine.*

The flickering lamp is furthermore our faltering life. We want to walk up the pathway of life with strength and courage, but again and again we stumble. It is harder going than we had expected. Jesus put out no spark of moral endeavor in anybody's life; he en- couraged. He said that he came not to take care of the righteous people who were all right already; he wished to help those who were sinners. He came to help not those that were well, but those that were sick, for they were the ones that needed a physician.

THE FLAME BURNS AGAIN

It is a wonderful thing when a smoking wick comes again into bright flame. One can never be sure that this cannot take place. It can transpire even in the last extremity. Two malefactors were to die with Jesus at the time of his crucifixion. One of them expired in bitterness of spirit and hardness of heart. As the other one, however, looked at the strange man upon the cross between them, something happened to him. A spark of hope and faith, which had almost been extinguished, revived within him. In new expectancy, he cried and said, "Jesus, remember me when you come in your kingly power." And Jesus said to a dying thief, "Today you will be with me in Paradise."[4] It was not even then too late.

This may happen in the most unlikely of places. Not long ago in Sing Sing prison, Louis Boy was serving out the eighteenth year of a life imprisonment. He was a condemned murderer. In the past eighteen years his hair had grown white, and he was now fifty years of age. Everything had changed in his life, and yet a spark within him had not entirely died. He heard about a little girl who was suffering with leukemia, a cancerous disease of the blood. He learned that there was a chance to help her if she might have an exchange of blood with a healthy person, but it would have to be vein to vein and it would mean that the disease would be introduced into the bloodstream of the person who ventured to make the exchange. No man had ever risked that. But Mr. Boy did. Something that had been sleeping for a long time in the heart of a man who had committed murder came to life and flamed up into the brilliance of a great heroism. With no promise of leniency or recompense he underwent the blood exchange. The little girl died despite what was done to try to help her, but when Christmas time came that year, Governor Thomas E. Dewey commuted the prisoner's life sentence to time already served, and Louis Boy walked out of Sing Sing a free man. He said, "This is the merriest Christmas I've ever had." As Browning put it:

> Beneath the veriest ash, there hides a spark of soul
> Which, quickened by love's breath, may yet pervade the whole
> O' the gray, and, free again, be fire.

Sometimes it is a bit of beauty that helps somebody so that the flame again comes to life. Florence Nightingale was desperately sick of fever in the Crimea. She left a record to the effect that it was the sight of a single rose which wooed her back to convalescence. More often, perhaps, it is love that helps somebody to want to live. A country doctor told the true story of John and Louise. John was a rancher, a strong, taciturn man. Louise was his wife. The doctor performed the operation when Louise experienced a burst appendix. Afterward she was desperately sick. Plasma was given twice, and still the pulse grew weaker and weaker. She said, "I'm just not strong enough." The doctor said, "I thought you said you were going to be big and strong like John." She replied, "John is so strong he doesn't need me." The doctor went to John and told him Louise did not want to get well. John said, "She's got to get well! How about a transfusion?" The doctor thought a bit, then took a sample of John's blood and typed it, and then he thought some more, but finally he said, "All right." As he gave the instructions to the nurse, he concluded with the words, "Neither of them has ever seen a transfusion." John lay on an operating table in her room, with a curtain between the two of them. There was a needle in his arm, and a needle in her arm. As the process went on, John said, "I'm going to make you well." She said, "Why?" He replied, "I need you." She said, "You never told me!" But the pulse began to get stronger, and when the doctor removed the needle and took the bottle of plasma out from under the towel and checked the pulse, it was steady and strong, and though she was still very sick he knew she was going to get well. He never told John that his blood had been of the wrong type and probably would have killed her if it had been given to her. It did not matter if it went into a bottle instead, and if another pint of plasma was administered to her. That which was given to her along with it was what revived the flickering spark of life.[5]

May we say in all reverence that Jesus Christ poured out his blood to revive the flickering spark of life within the heart of every man? It is a wonderful thing when a spark that is almost out is brought back to life again. Christ does that for men, and sometimes we too can help it to take place for somebody else.

MORE BEAUTIFUL THERE

At last, of course, the lamp of life will flicker and go out as far as human seeing is concerned, but if God has loved us as is shown in the tenderness of Jesus Christ, then we have good confidence to believe that the lamp of life will be brought to brightness in another world. In the book of Revelation, one of the visions is that of seven golden lampstands, with one like unto a Son of man in the midst of these. The lampstands are the seven churches, which stand for all the churches. The churches are made up of the people in them. Some of the people in those churches experienced martyrdom, but John saw the light of their life and faith shining more brightly than ever in the world beyond.

Thomas Edison helped us to advance beyond the little oil lamps of antiquity to the glorious brilliance of incandescent illumination in our time. When he who did so much to make this world brighter and lighter was dying, he stirred in his last heavy sleep and his attending physician, leaning close over him, heard his lips form the words, "It is very beautiful over there." The man who helped this world to be lighter and brighter seemed to catch a glimpse, before he died, of another still more radiant world. When the lamp of life flickers at last and goes out here, it will be brought back to a brighter brilliance by God who has shown us his gentleness and his care in the gentleness and care of Jesus Christ. He will not quench the smoking flax. The smoldering wick he will not put out.

CHAPTER THIRTEEN

The Night Cometh

A S THE life and work of Jesus went forward, opposition to him increased and the ominous threat of death began to be apparent. That his life would come to an end in suffering may have been evident to Jesus not only from the signs of gathering enmity but also from his study of prophetic passages in the Old Testament. The poems in Isaiah which described the gentleness of the Servant who would not quench a smoldering wick spoke also of his bearing the iniquity of many and of being wounded for the transgressions of others. At all events Jesus began to intimate to his disciples that the end was coming. One form in which this intimation was expressed is given in John 9:4: "We must work the works of him who sent me, while it is day; night comes, when no one can work." Although this statement begins in the first person singular in the Authorized Version based upon the late Byzantine text, "I must work the works of him that sent me," in the more ancient manuscripts it is phrased in the first person plural, "We must work the works of him who sent me," and thus justifies a consideration not only of Jesus' own sense of the approaching end but also of his teaching as to how every man should look toward the darkness.

Night and day have always made a deep impression upon mankind. "While the earth remaineth, seedtime and harvest, and cold and heat, and summer and winter, and day and night shall not cease."[1] This is written in the Bible, and so is many another word concerning day and night. "It must follow, as the night the day." This is in Shakespeare, and there is many another word in the poets about night and day in their inevitable succession. Man speaks of day and night not only in the literal meaning of these terms: twelve hours, more or less, of light, followed by twelve hours, more or less, of darkness; but also in a symbolical, figurative, metaphorical way. We speak of the day of life and the night of death. We speak of the day of human history and the night that will be the end of the world at the conclusion of all human history. Jesus was evidently using the words in some such way, going beyond their literal sense to their figurative meaning, when he said that he and his disciples must work the works of the One who had sent him while it was day, because the night was coming when no man can work.

WHEN WILL IT COME?

As man contemplates the coming of night, one of the first questions which arises in his mind is: When will the night come? Speaking of the literal day and night, we can answer that question with great accuracy. Most sportsmen make use of a table showing sunrise and sunset times. One can look at such a table and ascertain the exact hour and minute when the sun will go down any given night at a given latitude and longitude. Astronomers calculate the same figures far out into the future, centuries if you wish, and far back into the past, centuries back.

As the literal night comes at the end of the day, so it is equally certain that the night will come which is the end of the day of life and, according to every prophecy of the Bible, that the night will come which is the end of human history. But when these nightfalls will come, no one can tell. Some people think that we can trace out a particular line in the palm of the hand, and find the course of our life and the time of its ending, but this is of course not really so. Statistical tables are worked out which can tell us that if we are now of such and such an age, we have on the average so many years ahead of us. These tables are of such accuracy that great businesses are founded upon them, but they present averages only, and nobody can tell when the night is going to come for any individual person. That is hidden from us. Some people think that they can tell when the night will come which is the end of the world. Some believe that the great pyramid in Egypt is a prophecy in stone, and that by measuring its angles and inner passageways and chambers one can foresee all the periods in the history of the world, and when it is going to end. Others believe that by studying the prophecies in the Bible it is possible to construct a chart and know when the end will come. On this basis one small group of people was persuaded that the end of the world would take place on January 9, 1951. But we have already seen that Jesus Christ declined to say when the end would be. Only God knows about this certainty of nightfall, which from our point of view must remain as to time an utter uncertainty. It is the most certain thing in the world in its inevitable coming; it is the most uncertain thing in the world in our lack of knowledge as to when it will come.

THE TASKS OF THE DAY

A second question then arises: What must we do in the day, since the night is coming? To this there is a clear answer in what Jesus said. We must do the work that is given us to do while it is day, because the night is going to come. Jesus did that. At one time his life was threatened by Herod. This was Herod Antipas, the ruler of Galilee, the part of the country in which Jesus conducted most of his ministry. Antipas was a crafty, cunning, evil person. He stole his brother's wife and filled his reign with many evil deeds. He spoke of killing Jesus. People came and told the Master. He flung back the threat with these words: "Go and tell that fox [accurately characterizing Herod Antipas], 'Behold, I cast out demons and perform cures today and tomorrow, and the third day I finish my course.' "[2] With undisturbed spirit he went ahead doing the work of the day, in perfect confidence in the day, and with perfect fearlessness as to the night when it should at last come. Listen to the two quotations following, not so much to wonder if there is an implication of predestinarianism in them or not, as to sense the great faith which they express, a faith that when the end comes it will be within the providence of God and will be all right, and that up until that time everything will also be all right for the man who goes steadfastly ahead with his work. The first is a sentence by George Arthur Buttrick in his book, *Prayer,* and it is about Jesus. "He knew through prayer that God will keep a man until his word is spoken and his work is done, and that no brave man will ask God to stretch his breathing space beyond that day."[3] The second is a statement by Peter Marshall, and may be found in the collection of his sermons and prayers entitled *Mr. Jones Meet the Master.* He said, "When the clock strikes for me, I shall go, not one minute early, and not one minute late. Until then, there is nothing to fear."[4]

It is related of St. Francis of Assisi that he was hoeing his garden when somebody came by and asked him what he would do if he were suddenly to learn that at sunset that day he would die. The reply of St. Francis was: "I would finish hoeing my garden." That is a very good example for us all who live under the shadow of an uncertain future. We may not know what that future will bring, but we do know what task we have to perform in the present. The performing of the present task is the best preparation for the future, no matter what it may be.

Because the night is coming we must not only do our work in the day but also enjoy the day. The participation of Jesus in social affairs and the obvious joy which he and his disciples shared scandalized many. On one occasion he was asked why his disciples did not fast, as those of John and the Pharisees did. His reply was to ask whether it was to be expected that the wedding guests would fast while the bridegroom was with them? "The days will come," he said, with clear allusion to his own ultimate death, "when the bridegroom is taken away from them, and then they will fast on that day."[5] Until then, joy was appropriate.

A few years ago the following haunting story was reported by a correspondent from Canada. It had to do with two young ladies on the Gaspé Peninsula. They had cared for their widowed father and at his death had received a small legacy. The younger, Louise, suggested that they take a trip and see some of the places they had read about. The older, Miriam, thought that there was not enough money. They started a store and, being both attractive and energetic, made a great success of it. A number of years had gone by when a tourist car from Florida stopped. They looked at the license, and after the car was gone Louise proposed that they take a month's vacation and go to Florida, but Miriam was afraid that trade would go elsewhere if they went away. Ten years passed, and they had enough money to last them the rest of their lives. Louise suggested they might sell the store and take a trip to California, perhaps to Mexico. But Miriam thought no one would pay as much as the store was worth. Then the war came, and they worked harder than ever. One cold January, Louise started home alone from the store at night, across a field. She fell, suffered a fracture, and was not found until morning. Contracting pneumonia, she died in three days. Miriam never went back to the store. The funeral of her sister was the most impressive that area of the Gaspé had ever seen; there was a bronze coffin. When spring came, the authorities received a strange request. Permission was asked to move the body to California. Some months later, there was a new request for a disinterment permit. The bronze coffin went to Mexico City. The last the correspondent had heard about it, it was on its way to Havana. The one who wrote the account said: "It seems reasonable to assume that somewhere in the world today an uneasy coffin is resting in a fresh grave, and that not far from the cemetery a rich old lady is rocking away on a hotel porch, wondering what place her little sister would like to visit next."[6]

We must be kind to those around us while it is day, because the night comes and then we no longer have the opportunity. Home is sometimes where we treat worst those we like best. The sorrow of the loss of a dear one is not an insuperable one, being assuaged by many a remembrance of great happiness, unless there is mingled with it too much of regret and remorse. The only time to do anything about that is not after the night has fallen, but now, while the day is at hand.

It is also only in the time before night falls that it is possible for

us to improve the pathway for those who will come after. This is
illustrated by the poem of Will Allen Dromgoole, "The Bridge
Builder":

> *An old man going a lone highway*
> *Came in the evening cold and gray*
> *To a chasm vast and deep and wide.*
> *The old man crossed in the twilight dim,*
> *The sullen stream had no fears for him,*
> *But he stopped when safe on the other side*
> *And built a bridge to span the tide.*
>
> *"Old man," said a fellow pilgrim near,*
> *"You are wasting your strength with building here;*
> *Your journey will end with the ending day,*
> *You never again will pass this way,*
> *You've crossed the chasm deep and wide,*
> *Why build you this bridge at evening tide?"*
>
> *The builder lifted his old gray head,*
> *"Good friend, in the path I have come," he said,*
> *"There followeth after me today*
> *A youth whose feet must pass this way.*
> *This chasm which has been as naught to me*
> *To that fair-haired youth might a pitfall be,*
> *He, too, must cross in the twilight dim,*
> *Good friend, I am building the bridge for him."*[7]

We must mold the statue of life more finely while it is day, for
the night is coming when we will no longer be able to work at this
task. The Bible says that God made man out of the dust of the
earth. Then, however, he left man to do further shaping of that
dust of the earth, in the molding of his own life. Professor William
E. Hocking, one of whose books is entitled *What Man Can Make
of Man,* has said that we have a creative, reflective self, deep
within ourselves, and it is engaged constantly in the shaping of the
exterior, outward self. Finally comes the striking of the great gong
of passage which signals the going of the creative self to an ampler
field of work, and at that point the made self, the created self, is
left behind here as a permanent part of the fabric of history. Many
of us find that there are still some rough spots in the statue, still

some unsatisfactory places in the clay. Now and only now is the time to work further at the self we will someday leave behind.

We must make our life right with God while it is day, because the night comes. When we enter into the night, God will be there. According to the Bible, the night and the day are both alike to God. To him, even the night will be light, and if we know him it will not be utter darkness to us.

AFTER THE NIGHT

And what comes after the night? By the analogy of the comparison, where there is the day of work, the night that comes at the end of it will be followed by the morning beyond.

> *So shall it be at last, in that bright morning,*
> *When the soul waketh, and life's shadows flee;*
> *O in that hour, fairer than daylight dawning,*
> *Shall rise the glorious thought, I am with Thee.*

CHAPTER FOURTEEN

He Took It Upon Himself

ALTHOUGH Jesus anticipated death at the hands of his enemies, and spoke of the approach of night as we have just
seen, it would be incorrect to think of him as a helpless
victim. Throughout life his actions appear to be those, not of
a pawn, but of a person proceeding according to his own voli-
tion and with a clear understanding of consequences and ends.
If he carried loads and bore suffering, it was of his own free
choice.

At the end of a winter afternoon, Margaret Slattery was clear-
ing her desk preparatory to going home. Taking one last glance to
see that everything was in order, she noticed a torn magazine sheet
lying in the wastebasket. Printed in black and red type was a large
advertisement with these prominent words, "He Took It Upon
Himself." Thinking at first that it was a statement from the New
Testament, it seemed to her strange that it should be there in an
advertisement. Then she looked more closely and found in finer
type the story back of the phrase. A man had seen the need for a
new automobile tire. He had engaged in a series of experiments
and performed much labor in order to perfect this tire. The advertisement explained that he took it upon himself to try to make
that new tire, and that as a result of his long effort the tire had
been perfected and was now being offered to the buying public.
"He took it upon himself" and as a result such and such a tire
"has solved the problem for you," is what the advertisement declared.

WHAT JESUS DID

Although the words "he took it upon himself" are not to be found in that exact form in the New Testament, they seem very close to the spirit of the New Testament. Here are several points in the life of Christ which are rather accurately described by the phrase. For one thing, he took upon himself the support of his family. The family of Jesus included Joseph and Mary, of whom we read in the first two chapters of Matthew and of Luke, Jesus himself, four brothers whose names are given in Mark 6 and in Matthew 13, James, Joses, Judas, and Simon, and at least two sisters who are referred to in the plural without their names being given, in those same passages in Mark and Matthew. Joseph himself lived at least until Jesus was twelve years of age, for when he was twelve the family went to Jerusalem and Jesus became immersed in discussion with the wise men in the Temple, and in telling about that journey the parents, in the plural, are mentioned. Joseph, therefore, lived at least that long, maybe somewhat longer. But sometime after Jesus was twelve years of age, Joseph must have died, because after that time he appears no more in the gospel narrative. Joseph himself was a carpenter, according to Matthew 13:55 where the question stands about Jesus when he came back to Nazareth during his public ministry, "Is not this the carpenter's son?" They evidently meant, "He is just an ordinary person, is he not?" Jesus himself probably learned the trade of a carpenter from Joseph. This was in accordance with general Jewish custom. It is also attested by the other form of this same question in Mark 6:3 where they ask disparagingly about Jesus as he comes back to Nazareth, "Is not this the carpenter?" Therefore we conclude that when Joseph died Jesus, as the oldest son, continued the carpenter trade at Nazareth as the chief support of his own family. Remembering that even at the age of twelve he said, "I must be in my Father's house"[1] and was intensely interested in the Temple in Jerusalem, and that any young man naturally desires to be out in life for himself, we realize that there was renunciation involved in this. Nevertheless he took upon himself the support of his own family, and carried this responsibility until the beginning of his public ministry which, according to Luke, was when he was around thirty years of age.[2]

Jesus also took upon himself the form of a servant. Now we come to the words in the New Testament that are nearest, verbally, to those of our extra-Biblical quotation. According to Philippians 2:7 in the Authorized Version, Paul said in describing Christ: "He took upon him the form of a servant." In Greek the word servant is of course the same as the word slave. He took upon him the form of a slave. Paul declares that Jesus could have grasped after equality with God himself, but he did not do it. He humbled himself to the point that he made himself like unto a slave. In an incident narrated in John 14, Jesus did that literally. It was at the Last Supper, when the disciples and Jesus came to an upper room to eat their last meal together. Upon such an occasion in Palestine it was customary, where there was a host and a fine home, that a slave be provided to wash the feet of those who came. The paths of Palestine are dusty and the streets are dirty today; they must have been so then. Men walked along them in sandaled feet; there was nothing more refreshing for a guest than to come in and have a slave wash his feet upon arrival. But when Jesus and his disciples came to the last supper that they would eat together, there was no slave provided for them. Nor did any one of the disciples condescend to perform such a menial task for his associates. They had indeed just been engaged in an argument as to who was greatest among them. Thereupon Jesus took a towel and girded himself, and began to wash his disciples' feet. This was the act of a slave in the house, and he did it for his own followers. All the way through his life he took upon himself the form of a servant and did things to serve other people. "He came not to be served but to serve."[3]

Furthermore, he took upon himself the suffering of the cross. As far as human wisdom could see, that was not necessary. The first time Jesus referred to the eventuality, Peter began to rebuke him and say it should not be so. In evaluating the circumstances connected with the crucifixion, we would say that Jesus did not have to leave Galilee and go to Jerusalem where his chief enemies were. There, he did not have to challenge them in the Temple, the seat of their power. At the Last Supper, he did not have to let Judas, bent on his mission of betrayal, slip out. After that, Jesus did not have to go back to the garden of Gethsemane; as John tells us, Judas knew the place where Jesus often met with his disciples.[4] All of this adds up to the fact that John gives us as a statement of Jesus about his own life: "No one takes it from me, but I lay it down of my own accord."[5] He took upon himself voluntarily the suffering of the cross.

Once again, he took upon himself the sins of the world. An unnamed prophet of the Old Testament whose words are preserved in the latter part of the book of Isaiah pondered deeply the problems and sin of the world. It seemed to him that the only way it could all be taken care of was for a suffering Servant to come and bear it, though he himself was innocent and guiltless. About that suffering Servant this prophet wrote: "Surely he hath borne our griefs, and carried our sorrows. . . . But he was wounded for our transgressions, he was bruised for our iniquities; the chastisement of our peace was upon him; and with his stripes we are healed. All we like sheep have gone astray; we have turned every one to his own way; and the Lord hath laid on him the iniquity of us all."[6] Never until Jesus Christ came were those words adequately fulfilled, though the prophet may have hoped at first that his very nation would fulfill that picture. Jesus Christ came and took upon himself the sins of the world, as that suffering Servant was pictured as doing. He was not a military Messiah conquering the earth, nor a transcendent Messiah judging the world in a fiery last Assize; he was a suffering Messiah who bore the sins of other people. He was guiltless—he had done nothing wrong. Because of that, he was the one who could take up the sins of the world and carry them.

PRINCIPLES

Now let us try to enunciate several principles which are evident in what Jesus did. The first is the principle of primary responsibility. Some people in Jesus' day took minor responsibilities upon themselves and by doing so dodged more fundamental ones about which they ought to have been concerned. Jesus observed behavior of this kind and rebuked it in connection with the commandment, "Honor your father and your mother." A means had been devised whereby this obligation could be circumvented and avoided, and a person not have to do anything for his father and his mother, under the very guise of doing something for God. In tradition it was taught that if a man told his father or his mother, "What you would have gained from me is Corban (that is, given to God)," then he was no longer permitted to do anything for his father or mother. Evidently what happened was that a man who was at outs with his own parents, and did not want to take care of them, would say that he dedicated his property to God. He would speak over it this magic word, Corban—"given to God." Then perhaps he would have to turn some of it over to the Temple, or perhaps not, but all of it was henceforth taboo. Henceforth he had no responsibility to use any of his possessions on behalf of his needy father and mother. He had neatly eluded his duty by taking upon himself something which was, in those circumstances, quite secondary. The principle that we see in the fact that Jesus took the support of his own family upon himself is the principle of putting a primary responsibility in primary place. A pathetic article has described the forgotten men in veterans' hospitals. In many cases those who were heroes upon the battlefield are helpless now, and have been abandoned by their nearest kin who, though in some cases they live not far away, never come to see them. One such lad simply turned over and died in his loneliness, for no one ever came. Someone is avoiding a primary responsibility, and it does not seem to matter very much how many secondary responsibilities one fulfills and boasts about if one dodges the primary one.

Another principle that we observe is that of the obligation involved in having strength. This refers to any kind of strength. Whether it is strength of body, of mind, of financial position, or whatever it is, it carries with it obligation and responsibility. Jesus said, "Every one to whom much is given, of him will much be required."[7] Paul said, "We who are strong ought to bear the burdens that the weak make for themselves and us."[8] If a person has a position of privilege, then along with it goes a responsibility and an obligation. When Queen Victoria, who became a very great queen indeed, was but a twelve-year-old girl, her governess tried to show her the responsibility that she was going to bear in the future. She spoke of the weighty problems of the British Empire, and the trust which would be reposed in her upon her eighteenth birthday. When the child realized what it all meant, she burst into tears, threw her arms around her governess, and cried: "I *will* be good. I understand now why you have wished me to study and learn. So much will depend on me. Oh, I will be good!"

Also there is the principle of the cost of following Christ. He who took up the cross said that if any man would come after him he must also bear the cross. Surely a faith which meant crucifixion for its Leader should not be expected to be a bed of flowers for a disciple.

And there is the principle of vicarious suffering. While the word "vicarious" is not in the Bible, it is helpful in explaining the Bible. It refers to an action on behalf of or as representing another, an action performed or suffered by one person with results accruing to the benefit of another. In the moral realm there are some things which the guilty cannot do; only the innocent can act, with suffering, to redeem the guilty.

MODERN EXAMPLES

In the lives of modern followers of Jesus there are many examples of what it means to take something upon oneself. Here are two narrated by Margaret Slattery out of her own experience, and to be found in her book already cited.

A young girl, face flushed, hat in one hand and suitcase, falling open, in the other, staggered into the ladies' waiting room of a city railroad station. No matron was present, and when the girl spoke to any of the women sitting there or took her place beside them, they withdrew. Reeling from side to side, the girl burst into sentimental song. As her face was turned it was seen to be so young that it showed traces of real beauty. Then a Salvation Army girl came in to ask for contributions. Comprehending the situation at a glance, she greeted the girl, talked with her in a friendly way, helped her wash her face and gather her belongings, and then went with her to the ticket office. A woman who followed asked where the girl lived, and the Army girl gave the name of a small town twenty miles away. Another asked who would take care of the girl at that destination. "I am going with her," answered the member of the Salvation Army quietly. The misfortune and sin which all the others had only looked at, the girl of the Salvation Army had taken upon herself.

Up the hill, past Miss Slattery's own home, a ten-year-old girl used to hurry on Saturday afternoons. She was on her way to her Sunday School teacher's house, and on one occasion her eyes sparkled with special joy, for she was to stay for supper. It was no wonder that this was a matter of such delight, for as Miss Slattery learned later the little girl's own home was only two rooms in a basement. Much of the time her father was in the county jail because of his cruel treatment of his family when intoxicated. The mother went out to work and the child cared for four younger children and did the housework. Despite these surroundings, under the guidance of the Sunday School teacher, the little girl grew up to graduate from high school and normal school, to teach successfully for several years, and finally to marry and make a happy home in which a younger brother also found a place of refuge. "It costs to take upon oneself the burden of such a child," wrote Miss Slattery, "*of course* it costs. One of the other teachers in that Sunday School had said, 'I am willing to teach on Sunday but I can't be bothered by children running to my home during the week. It is too much to be expected of any teacher.' And it is truly 'too much to be *expected*' but not too much to be *given,* when once the call sounds in one's soul."[9]

CHAPTER FIFTEEN

Christ and Jerusalem

A T THE end of his ministry Jesus paid a last visit to Jerusalem. So significant were the events that transpired at that time and place that the gospel writers devote a relatively large proportion of space to their recital. In Mark, for example, six out of a total of sixteen chapters are given to the last few days in Jerusalem. By studying the attitude of Jesus toward the city and what he did there, we may hope to understand better his relation to our world.

SORROW

First of all, as he came to the city he wept over it. The modern road from Jericho to Jerusalem, like the ancient one, brings you around the shoulder of the Mount of Olives. Suddenly the holy city bursts upon your sight. The corner of the city nearest to you across the valley of the Kidron was, in the days of Jesus, occupied by the glorious Temple. A great program of reconstruction had been inaugurated by Herod the Great and was still continuing in the time of Jesus. The work of rebuilding was being done on a scale and with a magnificence which made the disciples cry, "Look, Teacher, what wonderful stones and what wonderful buildings!"[1] A common proverb of the day said, "He who has not seen Herod's building has never seen anything beautiful." Thus the sight of the city surely should have evoked patriotic pride, religious fervor, and national enthusiasm.

125

But "when he drew near and saw the city he wept over it." Why? Because Jerusalem had chosen the things of war instead of peace, and Jesus could see the tragedy that was coming. It was probably in A.D. 30 when Christ wept over the city. In A.D. 66 the Jewish war broke out, an "utterly hopeless, and therefore unreasonable and disastrous struggle," as Schuerer has called it. In the summer of A.D. 70 Jerusalem was besieged and conquered by Titus and the Roman armies. Battering rams hammered against Jerusalem's walls; earthworks surrounded it; and the starving poor people who slipped out to look for food were caught by the Romans and crucified in sight of the city. Within the walls famine reached a terrible height. Young men wandered about like shadows; the sewers were searched for food; shoes were chewed on for sustenance; and a woman devoured her own child. Finally the city fell amidst indiscriminate slaughter; flames leaped across the beautiful Temple; and Jerusalem was razed to the ground.

Could Jesus have foreseen that? Certainly! If Lloyd George could say in 1919 that what they did at Versailles about Poland would "lead sooner or later to a new war in the east of Europe," of course the penetrating mind of Jesus could perceive the course of events in his day. This is the full record as given by Luke:

> And when he drew near and saw the city he wept over it, saying, "Would that even today you knew the things that make for peace! But now they are hid from your eyes. For the days shall come upon you, when your enemies will cast up a bank about you and surround you, and hem you in on every side, and dash you to the ground, you and your children within you, and they will not leave one stone upon another in you; because you did not know the time of your visitation."[2]

Will he not then be weeping for our world today? I believe that he weeps for all those who are involved in the terrible consequences of man's warfare and stupidity: the displaced and homeless, the sick and starving, the refugees and all who are in despair. During the war in Korea this description was contained in a dispatch printed in the *New York Times:* "Close behind the front pitiful columns of refugees were making their way in the hope of reaching safer territory farther south. Besides suffering from cold and malnutrition most of them were also soaked to the skin. Too terrified to stop and seek shelter, they were frequently under fire from both sides."[3] From Berlin, Germany, came this picture of the people in the congregation of one pastor: "For twenty years violence has ridden over their lives. Many have become doubtful about God, without quite being able to deny him—else they would not be in church. And when one speaks to the younger generation about the love of God, the answer is a shrug of the shoulders. They point to the ruins that surround the church. They tell the story of their family: the father perished in a concentration camp; a brother was killed in battle . . . the family dwelling was bombed to ruins. For five years they have not had a home fit for a human being; at work they are constantly spied on. The love of God? They have never known what that is."[4]

But when we remember the sorrow of Christ for Jerusalem we can at least answer the question whether all of this is the will of God with the conviction that first of all it is a tragedy in which he shares our grief. Jesus wept over Jerusalem, and as H. R. Mackintosh said in his *Doctrine of the Person of Jesus Christ,* "The tears of Jesus are the pity of God."

WRATH

But Jesus was also angry with Jerusalem. If one reads straight on in the passage from Luke which we quoted above one finds these words, "And he entered the temple and began to drive out those who sold."[5] Mark has preserved a slight but significant variation in the narrative at this point. He relates that it was already evening when Jesus entered the Temple and looked round about on everything. The indignation that flamed in the Master's heart as he saw the corruption in the sacred Temple did not explode in precipitate action. He went away. He returned the next morning with steadfast purpose and, one man against the many, drove out the money-changers and the buyers and sellers. In his upraised hand, according to John, was "a whip of cords."[6]

Shall we not say that the indignation of Jesus is the wrath of

God? More than once in the New Testament it is stated that Jesus was moved with indignation or anger.[7] Many times both in the Old Testament and the New Testament the "wrath of God" is mentioned. This does not mean an anthropomorphic conception of God as having a bad temper. It does mean what Paul said: "Do not be deceived; God is not mocked, for whatever a man sows, that he will also reap."[8] It means that a day of tragedy may also be a day of judgment. It means something similar to what Abraham Lincoln said in the solemn words of the Second Inaugural:

> Fondly do we hope—fervently do we pray—that this mighty scourge of war may speedily pass away. Yet, if God wills that it continue until all the wealth piled by the bondman's two hundred and fifty years of unrequited toil shall be sunk, and until every drop of blood drawn with the lash shall be paid by another drawn by the sword, as was said three thousand years ago, so still it must be said: "The judgments of the Lord are true and righteous altogether."

In *Days of Our Years,* Pierre van Paassen told a story which illustrates something of the kind of indignation of which we are speaking. In a French village where van Paassen was then living dwelt a hunchback named Ugolin. He was a remarkable man with a love for good music and a dignity which required that he work to support himself. But one night on his way home through the streets of the village he ran into a crowd of people in a hilarious mood, some drunk. Someone jostled Ugolin and he fell to the street and could not rise. They began to dance about him, kicking him, stepping on his fingers, shouting vile epithets, and singing a song about his unfortunate sister. Then they tied him to a lantern post, tore his clothes from him, and yelled and screamed and laughed. It was then that the parish priest, the Abbé de la Roudaire, came along. Although he was an aged man of eighty years he found the strength to cut Ugolin free and carry him away in his arms to his own home. The next morning while the priest was at Mass, the hunchback got up, walked to the river, and drowned himself. When his sister learned the news, she shot herself. Pierre van Paassen went to see the Abbé that evening, scarcely daring to ask if the suicides would at least have a decent Christian burial. The Abbé, however, assured him that they would, and said that they were not suicides but children who had been murdered by a society without mercy. On the day of the funeral it seemed as if the entire village was crowded into the church. When the Abbé mounted the pulpit he stood there for a moment, looking at the congregation intently, and turning his head from left to right slowly as if he wished to recognize every man and woman present. Then he addressed the people as "Christians," and when he said the word it had the sound of a whiplash. He went on to tell them that on the day of Judgment when the Lord would ask him where his sheep were, he would not be able to answer. And when the Lord would press him for an answer he would finally have to reply that they were not sheep but a pack of wolves.[9]

Even so the Great Shepherd must look down upon his people and his followers today as they war and strive with one another, and feel that they are not sheep but wolves.

LOVE

Yet Jesus also loved Jerusalem and sought till the end to win its people to himself. In the same way he still wants to help us. If we said only that Christ weeps, someone would call him sentimental. If we said only that he is angry, someone would feel that he is harsh. Truly he weeps with those that weep in the tragedies of our times. Certainly his righteousness is not to be mocked; the rod of his righteous judgment is upon us. But his sorrow and his wrath are mingled in his love. Because of that, a day of tragedy and of judgment is also a day of opportunity. His strong hands, which once held his head as he wept and again were uplifted in indignation in the Temple court, at last were outstretched upon the cross as if to gather all men to himself.

It is still and always, therefore, a day of opportunity for the world, even as Studdert-Kennedy said during the first World War: "Through the vast complexities of our modern civilized world made one by God, the crucified Christ is looking down upon us with death in his bleeding hands and feet but life in his burning eyes and demanding from us all, every individual man and woman, a choice between the glory of Reason, Patience, Love, and the glory of Force, Wrath and Fear. He will not go away. I do not believe he will let us alone. He is making us waver all over the world. He is going to drive us to a decision with his wounded hands. He will not let us have his world for a playground, a battlefield, a factory, or an empire any longer; we must give it to him. We must give it to him or there will be darkness over the world from the sixth to the ninth hour—and that may be for a thousand years."

It is also still a day of opportunity for the individual. In any day we can play our part as men. If it is given us to share in the sufferings of our time, we can in that way render back to Christ a fraction of his sacrifice for us. In a poem by Joyce Kilmer, which George Stewart printed in *The Crucifixion in Our Street,* a soldier was pictured who, though weighed down with fatigue in France, found his own life and strength renewed in the contemplation of Christ's sufferings. With shoulders aching beneath his pack, feet burning as he marched, salty drops searing his eyes, and hand stiff and numb, he cried:

> *Lord, Thou didst suffer more for me*
> *Than all the hosts of land and sea.*
>
> *So let me render back again*
> *This millionth of Thy gift. Amen.*[10]

CHAPTER SIXTEEN

Lord, Is It I?

O N THE last evening of his life, Jesus ate a last supper with
his disciples. While they were eating, he said that one
of them was going to betray him. When they heard this
announcement they became very sorrowful and began to say to
him, one after another, "Is it I, Lord?"[1]

IN INDIVIDUAL LIFE

It was to their credit that the disciples asked this question. It
meant that each was interrogating himself first of all. It would have
been very easy for the disciples to ask the question, each one about
his neighbor. We know that they bickered and quarreled among
themselves. There was rivalry and jealousy. It would have been
very easy for each disciple to turn to his neighbor, in his thoughts
at any rate, and say in effect, "Lord, is it he who is going to betray
you?" They might have pointed that finger of suspicion at James
and John. James and John had recently asked Jesus if they might
have the chief places at his right hand and his left hand when he
came into his kingdom, and Jesus had declined to tell them that
they could have the places. They might, therefore, have been dis-
gruntled. The other disciples were of course displeased with them
for their thinking that they were so pre-eminent. So they might
have said, "Lord, is it James?" "Lord, is it John?" Or they might
have said, "Lord, is it Peter?" Peter always stepped forward, always
spoke up, always took the lead. Sometimes we are suspicious and

131

jealous of leaders, and secretly hope that they will trip and fall. The disciples might have questioned about Peter. They might have said, "Lord, is it Judas?" He was the treasurer for the group. He held the moneybag. Sometimes people are suspicious of those who control the funds. They might have pointed the finger at Judas, and asked either aloud or within themselves, "Lord, is he the one?" If they had done so, in that case they would have been right. Judas was going to betray Jesus. But they were finer men for not having stated that question, for having asked instead, each one, "Lord, is it I?" They interrogated themselves first of all. That is a good thing to do.

It is also good that the disciples asked this question because it means that they were judging themselves before they judged others. It is always easier to judge another person than to judge ourselves. It is always easier to recognize sin when somebody else commits it than when we do. In the Old Testament we read about King David. He looked upon Bathsheba and took her, and caused her husband, Uriah the Hittite, to be put in the front line of battle, so that he was killed. Nathan the prophet came to King David and told him a story. There were two men in a city, the story began; one was a rich man, the other was a poor man. The rich man had many herds and flocks. The rich man's neighbor, the poor man, had one little ewe lamb. A guest came to the rich man's house, and since he wished to provide a fine banquet for him, he had the poor man's lamb seized and slain to provide the main dish for the meal. By this time David became very angry and said that the man was worthy of death and should be compelled to restore fourfold. Then Nathan said, "Thou art the man." To David's credit, he recognized that it was a picture of himself and said, "I have sinned,"[2] which is always the beginning of restoration. It was much easier to see that somebody else had done something wrong than to recognize and acknowledge that he himself had done so. Jesus put the matter in the striking question, "Why beholdest thou the mote that is in thy brother's eye, but considerest not the beam that is in thine own eye?" If by any chance this language of the King James Version seems obscure, read the same verse in Moffatt's vivid translation: "Why do you note the splinter in your brother's eye and fail to see the plank in your own eye?"[3] As Halford E. Luccock says, we all know what a splinter is; we run them into our fingers. Sometimes they are so tiny we can hardly see them to get them out. As for a plank, we know what that is, too; a plank of wood is big enough to stop a street car.[4] Jesus said also, "Judge not, that you be not judged."[5] Leslie D. Weatherhead remarks that by judging others we give ourselves away to anyone with insight, revealing ourselves as people who should ourselves be judged. The pleasure we experience at the fall of another ministers to our own complacency and makes us feel that after all we are not so bad. "At any rate, dear," said a man to his wife in Dr. Weatherhead's presence, as he passed over the evening paper that told about the downfall of a rival, "we haven't fallen to *that!*"[6] So he judged himself in judging another. The condemnation we express of what another does may show the hidden desire within ourselves. Psychologists state, as Weatherhead also points out, that when they hear someone use very strong language in speaking of some particular sin, they conclude that that is the temptation which is the strongest threat and greatest danger to the speaker himself. He condemns another for the fault that is his own particular weakness. So it is good that the disciples, instead of passing judgment, each on the other, questioned and passed judgment each upon himself.

It is also a good thing that the disciples asked this question because it means that they were examining themselves and were recognizing that they did not know what they were capable of doing. Why did the disciples, each one, say, "Lord, is it I?" Did not each one know if he would do this act or not? When the circle was completed and the question went all the way around, and Judas said, "Lord, is it I?" of course he knew. According to the gospel record, he had already made his bargain with the priests. He had already received his thirty pieces of silver. He was only waiting for an opportune time to turn Jesus over to his enemies. So when Judas said to Jesus, "Lord, is it I?" he was saying it dishonestly. But what about the others? Did not each one know whether he were going to betray Jesus or not? No, they did not know. Often a man does not know what he is capable of doing. Jeremiah said, "The heart is deceitful above all things, and it is exceedingly corrupt: who can know it?"[7] We do not know what we may do in a sudden crisis. Consider the overconfidence and the downfall of Peter that same night. Jesus said to his disciples, I think more in sorrow than in condemnation, "You will all fall away because of me this night." He quoted Zechariah, "I will strike the shepherd, and the sheep of the flock will be scattered."[8] He, the shepherd, was going to be smitten and his sheep, the disciples, were going to be scattered. But Peter, the big fisherman who had sailed his ship across the storms of Galilee and had never been afraid of anything, said, "Though they all fall away because of you, I will never fall away." Jesus knew him better than he knew himself. Jesus said to him, "Before the cock crows, you will deny me three times."[9] Before the sky grows light with the morning and the herald of the morning sends out his call, Peter will three times deny that he knows Jesus. Peter did not think it could possibly happen. When Jesus was taken away into the palace of the high priest, Peter was indeed braver than any of the rest. He followed as far as within the courtyard. There he sat by the fire, warming himself and engaging perhaps in small talk to make it appear as if he were just one of the others. A young woman thought she recognized him and asked him if he had not been with Jesus. Peter said that he did not know what she meant. Later another young woman brought it up again, and again Peter denied it, saying that he did not even know the man. Later the bystanders asked if he did not belong to the followers of Christ, and declared that his Galilean accent betrayed him, but Peter denied it with an oath. Then the cock crowed. Peter remembered, and realized, and went out and wept bitterly. Not until his later threefold affirmation of love for Christ was this failure canceled out.

We do not always know what we are capable of doing in the longer drift of life. It is said that when Leonardo da Vinci was making his famous painting of the Last Supper, he sought out models for the various persons who were to be shown in it, and of all thirteen men who were to appear in the picture, he had difficulty in finding persons for only two representations—Jesus and Judas. In a Milan cathedral choir he found a fine young man for his model to paint the face of Christ in the picture. Then it was some years before he finally found the person to serve as model for the face of Judas. This was a convict in a Roman prison. When he became acquainted with this man he was appalled to find that he was none other than the youth who, a few years before, sat for the face of Christ. The story may be only apocryphal, but it is really no stranger than what happened to Judas himself. He started out with great enthusiasm as a follower of Christ. He ended up hanging himself in utter shame, Christ's betrayer. It is a good thing to ask the question, "Lord, is it I?" because we do not know what we are capable of doing.

Once again, it is a good thing to ask this question, as the disciples did, because when we do it we open ourselves to the help of Christ. His help may be unable to get through to us as long as we are perfectly confident and sure that we can do everything by ourselves. We will never make any mistake. We will never stumble. We will never get into any trouble. We will never do anything we are ashamed of. As long as we are so good as all that, Christ's help may not be able to get through to us. But when we say, "Lord, is it I?" then we are putting ourselves where Christ's help can reach us. This is the way it was for the disciples at that supper. They asked the question in all honestness and then a little later Jesus was handing them the bread, he was passing them the cup, he was saying: "This is my body. This is my blood poured out for the forgiveness of sins."[10] What do we need so much as this? There he was, offering them forgiveness and giving his own life to make it possible. They were able to receive it because they were humble. They never forgot that hour, and afterward when they ate together, the broken bread was still his body, and the cup his blood. Ere long, as we read in the book of Acts,[11] they did this on the first day of the week, every Sunday. That is why, on every Sunday or on an appointed Sunday, the Lord's Supper is still observed in the churches. At it, there is an invitation and an offer—an offer of strength and help, and when we come humbly, that help reaches us.

IN THE CHURCH

It is also appropriate that this same question be asked in the church itself. Sometimes the church has not realized what it is capable of doing. Kirby Page once wrote a book called *Jesus or Christianity*.[12] He called it "a study in contrasts," and the entire book was occupied with examples of differences between the teaching and spirit of Jesus Christ and the actions and attitudes of the church across the centuries. One may cite the example of the Inquisition when, for several centuries, torture was used systematically by the Christian church in dealing with heretics. One could hardly believe that a thing like that would happen—and yet it did. All too often the churches and church people have judged harshly about small faults in others and have been oblivious to larger errors among themselves. In Virginia, at the same time that a man could be legally executed if he failed to go to church twice on Sunday and committed the same offense three times over, the slave trade was flourishing with the blessing of the church. In England in the Victorian era there was anxiety over the wickedness of playing the piano on Sunday, and lack of concern for the evils of child labor.

It is well, therefore, that in the church the question should often be asked, "Lord, is it I?" De we profess Christian love, and manifest smallness of attitude? Do we inveigh against sin, and commit sin? Do we believe in the oneness of all people, and yet approve denominational divisions among ourselves? When we ask the question we humble ourselves before the Lord of the church. All around the world today Christians are searching themselves in the spirit of humility, and by the influence of Christ the churches are being led toward a greater unity.

IN THE NATION

It also behooves us to ask this same question on behalf of our nation. "Lord, is it we?" In time of war and world strife, we emphasize our own righteousness and criticize the evil of others upon earth. But if other people did what we do, what would we call it? Would we call it imperialism? Would we call it militarism? Would we call it selfish enjoyment of luxury, heedless of the needs of others? If we grow proud and arrogant and go our own way, Christ cannot help us; but if we humble ourselves and seek for his guidance, his spirit can continue to lead the nation.

As a nation, as a church, and as individuals, it is well that we join the early disciples at the table of the Supper with Christ, and join them in asking the same question they asked. Then we are interrogating ourselves first; we are judging ourselves before we judge others; we are remembering that we do not know what we may be capable of; we are asking for help and placing ourselves where we may receive it, for whoever will ask for help will receive it, and strength, with the body and the blood of the Lord Jesus Christ.

CHAPTER SEVENTEEN

Father, Forgive Them

AS WE selected one word at the Last Supper for study, so we
select one word from the Cross. It is what Jesus said as he
was crucified, according to Luke 23:34: "Father, forgive
them; for they know not what they do."

THE DEED OF MEN

In these words is a true statement of how men came to do a great
evil. Men crucified Jesus because they did not know what they
were doing. They did not know who Jesus was. From the earliest
beginnings of his life, men did terrible things to him, because they
did not know who he was.

The Jewish people thought he was a false leader. The record
about Jesus in the Talmud reads: "On the eve of Passover they
hanged Yeshu. And an announcer went out in front of him saying:
'He is going to be stoned, because he practiced sorcery and en-
ticed and led Israel astray.'" The Romans thought he was a pre-
tender to a throne. They caused to be written above his head when
he was crucified the accusation, "The King of the Jews."[1] They
thought he was trying to set himself up as a king, and that meant
to perform an act of rebellion against their power. The soldiers who
crucified him did not know who he was; they thought he was a
criminal like the other two whom they had to execute that selfsame
day. As Paul put it later, "None of the rulers of this age understood

his; for if they had, they would not have crucified the Lord of glory."[2]

The men who were responsible for putting Jesus to death did not know that their earlier actions would result in their finally doing his thing. At first all they did was to resist his teachings. The scribes said about him, "Why does he eat and drink with tax collectors and sinners?"[3] They thought, "Anybody who does that is going to break down the social order, and ruin the caste system." The Pharisees said about Jesus and his disciples, "Why are they doing what is not lawful on the sabbath?"[4] They thought, "People acting that way are going to destroy our sacred laws." Thus they resisted his teaching first of all.

Then they went a step farther. They maligned his name. They said, "He is possessed by Beelzebub."[5] They declared that the reason he could cast out demons was that he was aligned with the prince of the demons. Then they went on eventually, having started out by only resisting his teaching and maligning his name, to attack his body and to put him to death. But they did not realize that those earlier actions were going to lead to that drastic and terrible and final thing.

There is even a theory that Judas did not realize what his action was going to result in. The theory runs like this: Judas thought that by putting Jesus into the hands of his enemies, he could force him to take an effective action at last. Jesus had unaccountably postponed his inauguration of the kingdom of God. Therefore turn him over to his enemies, and then he will have to act, show people who he is, and set up the kingdom of God. The theory is that Judas betrayed Jesus with that in mind; if so, he did not know what it was really going to lead to.

Those who crucified Jesus, furthermore, did not know how it was going to look afterward. The New Testament shows how it looked afterward to Judas; regardless of what ideas he may have had in mind ahead of time, we know that afterward his deed appeared to him as a terrible shame. When he saw it in its true light, he rushed out and hanged himself. We have from the poet John Masefield a description of how the crucifixion looked afterward to

Longinus, who was the centurion in charge of the soldiers that performed the act. In the poem, Longinus returns to report to Pilate, and Pilate asks, "What happened at the cross?" Longinus answers:

> *We nailed him there*
> *Aloft, between the thieves, in the bright air.*
> *The rabble, and the readers mocked with oaths,*
> *The hangman's squad were dicing for his clothes.*
> *The two thieves jeered at him. Then it grew dark,*
> *Till the noon sun was dwindled to a spark,*
> *And one by one the mocking mouths fell still. . . .*
> *There came a cry.*
> *Jesus was calling God: it struck us dumb.*
> *One said "He is calling God. Wait. Will God come?*
> *Wait." And we listened in the glare. O sir,*
> *He was God's son, that man, that minister,*
> *For as he called, fire tore the sky in two,*
> *The sick earth shook and tossed the cross askew,*
> *The earthquake ran like thunder, the earth's bones*
> *Broke, the graves opened, there were falling stones. . . .*
> *Jesus cried*
> *Once more and drooped, I saw that he had died.*
> *Lord, in the earthquake, God had come for him.*
> *The thought of it shakes me sick, my eyes are dim.*[6]

Men did not know the full enormity of what they were doing at the time they did it. Men committed a great evil without knowing how great the evil was that they were doing.

THE SPIRIT OF JESUS

In the words of Jesus there is also a true expression of the great spirit of Jesus Christ himself. All through his life he had taught people to forgive others. Peter asked, "How often shall my brother sin against me, and I forgive him?" Stretching his imagination as far as he could, he proposed that he do it seven times. Jesus said, "Seventy times seven."[7] Someone else may have asked Jesus whether religious worship is always effective. He replied that if you come to worship and have hate in your heart against your brother, it is of no avail. "First be reconciled to your brother, and then come and offer your gift."[8] He taught his disciples to pray, "Our Father who art in heaven. . . . Forgive us our debts, as we also have forgiven our debtors."[9] All through his life he had taught men to forgive, and now there comes this climactic expression of his great spirit as he himself prays, "Father, forgive them; for they know not what they do." James Gordon Gilkey comments thus: "When Jesus came to the crisis of His own life He heroically put into practice the principle He had been recommending so steadily to others. Think of the moments before the crucifixion. Two Roman soldiers are kneeling, one at the head and the other at the feet of Jesus. Hammers, and a pile of rusty iron spikes. Then, amid four flashes of agony, Jesus gasps, 'Father, forgive! They know not what they do.' Why did Jesus emphasize forgiveness so constantly? Why did He practice it Himself in one of the most unlikely situations imaginable? Because He knew what havoc bitterness—even justifiable bitterness—works in human hearts. He knew that He Himself must forgive if He were to endure the agony of Golgotha. Only when the last trace of resentment is swept away can a man meet the ultimate demands of life."[10]

Cunningham Geikie writes: "Racked by the extremest pain, and covered with every indignity which men were wont to heap on the greatest criminals; forsaken and denied by His disciples; no sigh escaped His lips, no cry of agony, no bitter or faltering word; only a prayer for the forgiveness of His enemies. . . . His prayer that His heavenly Father would pardon them was only a last utterance of the love of which He had been the embodiment and expression through life, and the fitting illustration of His words, that He came to call the sick, not those who had no need of a physician."[11]

HELP FOR MEN

Once more, the word which Jesus spoke is a true guide for us, to help us to keep from sinning, or to help us if we have sinned, or to help us if somebody has sinned against us. Let us look at those things, in that order.

This word is a help to us, to keep us from sinning. It shows us what a great evil men can do without being aware that they are performing such an enormity. Therefore we must ask ahead of time these questions: Who is the person whom we are hurting? They did not know who he was. Do we know who the person is, to whom we are doing some harm? Do we treat a little child cruelly? Who is he, in origin and in destiny? In origin, he is a spirit from God; in destiny, he is perhaps a great man of tomorrow. Who is the person that we are treating cruelly? His skin may be of another color than our own, but he is a child of God.

Again, what will the actions that we are doing now lead unto? S. Ralph Harlow, later Professor of Religion at Smith College, taught at one time in an American college in Turkey. One day on the streets of Smyrna, as he has related, a Greek policeman came to him and told him that an American boy was dying in a hospital in that city. He found a young American man in the last stages of delirium tremens. In his saner moments, he talked. Harlow learned that he was from a fine family back in Virginia. He had graduated from a leading university, and was a member of an important fraternity there. If his fraternity brothers could have heard what he said in the last days of his life, three days that were a continuous nightmare, they would have had unhappy thoughts the rest of their lives. It was in the fraternity that they had told him, "Another little drink won't do you any harm." And here was the end of the road. A telegram came from the American Embassy at Constantinople, asking that the consul in Smyrna try to trace a young man who had been heard of last at a Black Sea port. The request was from this man's mother and sister at home. The message arrived after the boy died, but from it they learned his name, which he had refused to tell. So his body went back home to the dead hopes of his family and perhaps past the door of the fraternity, where one more step along the road had not looked serious, but had led at last to this end.

How will what we propose to do look afterward? The cross

looked different after the deed was done. It looks different now in the light of history. A kidnapper and murderer said the other day, "I'm terribly sorry I did it, of course, but I can not really believe it happened." His mind rebelled against seeing that he had actually done the thing. Afterward, how different it looked from before.

There is help in these words to keep us from sinning, but there is also help in them if we have sinned. Jesus hung there upon the cross, where men had nailed him cruelly, and he prayed for them. Since he prayed for them, he will surely pray for us too. If we have sinned against others and against him, he will ask God to be kind to us, to look upon us tenderly and mercifully.

These two affirmations were expressed concisely in an early Christian letter: "My little children, I am writing this to you so that you may not sin; but if any one does sin, we have an advocate with the Father, Jesus Christ the righteous."[12] An advocate is one who pleads for you. We have such a one in Jesus Christ. There is help for us if we have sinned.

And there is help for us if someone has sinned against us. It is one of the hardest things in life to take, when someone else does us wrong, or speaks an unkind and insidious word against us. Afterward there often remains within us a smoldering anger, a continuing bitterness. Then that begins to destroy us. Quoting Gilkey again: "You want to know the real source of your unhappiness, your ineffectiveness, your flashes of uncontrollable bitterness and anger? Look honestly into your own heart. Do you hate anybody? Do you want to 'get even' with anybody? Is there anybody you would like to see suffer? If you can locate any such roots of bitterness you have found the hidden source of your spiritual troubles."[13]

A former mayor of New York, whom Dr. Gilkey mentions, was the object of vicious attacks by the yellow journals of the city, was bitterly satirized by his opponents, and was finally the victim of physical violence, being almost murdered by a maniac. He underwent a long convalescence in the hospital, and during that period he used to say: "Every night I forgive everything, everybody." "Gaining that spirit is one price of quiet and effective living," says Gilkey. Gaining that spirit is one part, too, of becoming a follower of Jesus Christ, this man who was there on the cross, and on that cross prayed to God, "Father, forgive them; for they know not what they do."

So there is help for us in this word. There is power to guide us in the way of righteousness rather than sin. There is pardon if we have sinned, for Jesus will ask God to forgive us, and what Jesus asks God, God will do. And there is peace, for we cannot ever have peace when we are bitter against somebody else. The only way we can ever have peace is to come as well as we can in our own way, perhaps even with faltering lips, saying those same words if anyone has done wrong to us: "Father forgive them; for they know not what they do."

Conclusion

CHAPTER EIGHTEEN

𝕴 𝖀𝖒 𝕯𝖊𝖇𝖙𝖔𝖗

THOSE WHO have learned to know about Jesus, and above all those who have heard his kindly prayer of forgiveness, have always felt a sense of obligation. It was expressed by Paul in the simple words, "I am debtor."[1]

I HAVE RECEIVED

To say that one is a debtor means that one has received something. From Jesus we have learned much about God, and know that we are debtors to him in that we have received much from him. Paul, the apostle of Jesus Christ, expresses in the opening section of Romans a sense of God's agelong purpose and of his own special part in it: "set apart for the gospel of God which he promised beforehand through his prophets in the holy scriptures, the gospel concerning his son."[2] Every one who believes in God according to the teachings of Jesus may have a feeling of the long-range purpose of God and of his own special place in that purpose. God has made here a beautiful world. In it he has established conditions favorable to life. Here he has not only brought forth life, but also lifted it to the level of self-consciousness, intelligence, and love. He has endowed us with certain abilities. He helps us to find a place where we can use these abilities. He permits us to see beautiful things, mountains, seas, lakes, forests, flowers, clouds, stars. He causes a multitude of things to work together for good in our lives, often beyond our dreaming and beyond our deserving.

When evil things transpire, he is still there, willing to work with us for good, to the end that in the long run something good may yet be wrought out. When we sin against him, he promises his forgiveness—and gives his forgiveness. It is entirely appropriate that we should say with the Psalmist of old: "Bless the Lord, O my soul, and forget not all his benefits: who forgiveth all thine iniquities; who healeth all thy diseases."[3]

We are also directly in debt to Jesus Christ. Paul speaks specially about him, "Jesus Christ our Lord, through whom we have received grace and apostleship."[4] If we know very much about the infinite, eternal God, it is because of Jesus Christ. If we have a clear sense of what God wants us to do, it is particularly because of Jesus Christ. When somebody does something for somebody else, the other person is indebted to him. Jesus has done very much for all the world. He has lived the best life that has ever been seen upon this planet. He has laid down his life in love for his friends, and for his enemies. We are indebted to him. He has shown us the way, as a guide leads upon a trail that goes toward a high goal. He has shown us truth about the moral and spiritual side of life, in particular. When we disregard this truth, all goes wrong; when we obey it, all goes well. He is like a gate to life. The gateway is narrow, but the path beyond it, instead of being a dead-end street, is one that broadens out into more abundant life. We are debtors to Jesus Christ.

We are debtors to the church, which is the collective association of the followers of Christ. As Paul writes, note his eager sense of anticipation. He is going to go to Rome. He is going to have association with the church there too. He looks forward to it as a thing that will mean mutual encouragement for them and for him. We too are indebted to the church. If it were not for the people of the church down across the centuries, we would not know anything about Jesus today. They have handed down the word, paid the price, done the work. Paul himself was one of those who did this. Edward Wilson, a member of the immortal company of men who died with Captain R. F. Scott in the Antarctic, as a younger man and a medical student, read the letter of Paul to the Romans. When he finished, he wrote the words, "Dear Apostle, we Gentiles are grateful to you." Indeed we are grateful to Paul the Jew for what he did, and to Augustine of North Africa, and Luther of Germany, and many others. We are also debtors to the church as it is around us now. It is in the church that teachers tell us about the Bible. It is in the church that ministers tell the story of Jesus. It is in the church that his followers are baptized, and married, and it is by the ministry of the church that they are buried. The familiar words of William Henry Boddy may be abbreviated thus:

> *Before I was born my church gave to my parents*
> *ideals of life and love . . .*
> *In childhood my church joined my parents in*
> *teaching me of Christ . . .*
> *My church enriched my childhood with the romance*
> *of religion and the lessons of life . . .*
> *In the stress and storm of youth my church . . .*
> *guided my footsteps by lifting my eyes toward*
> *the stars.*
> *When first my heart knew the strange awakenings*
> *of love, my church taught me to . . . spiritualize*
> *my affections.*
> *When my heart was seamed with sorrow, and I thought*
> *the sun could never shine again, my church drew*
> *me to the Friend of all the weary, and whispered*
> *to me the hope of another morning, eternal and*
> *tearless.*
> *When my steps have slipped and I have known the*
> *bitterness of sin, my church has believed in me*
> *and wooingly she has called me back to live*
> *within the heights of myself . . .*
> *My church calls me to her heart. She asks my*
> *service and my loyalty. She has a right to ask*
> *it! I will help her to do for others what she*
> *has done for me. In this place in which I live,*
> *I will help her keep aflame and aloft the torch*
> *of a living faith.*

We are debtor to other people. Paul said, "First I thank my God through Jesus Christ for all of you."[5] Before he finishes the letter he puts in a section in which he mentions as many people as he is

acquainted with in Rome with whom he has had contact elsewhere
in the world and in Christian work. He names Prisca and Aquila
"my fellow workers in Christ Jesus, who risked their necks for my
life"; Andronicus and Junias, "my fellow prisoners"; and many
others.[6]

We are in debt to the members of our families who have always
loved us and encouraged us. We are in debt to our faithful and
true friends, and to our fellow workers. In the Lord's Prayer, we
are taught to pray that our debts may be forgiven as we forgive our
debtors, in the sense of those who have transgressed against us.
Some of us would find it difficult to think of very many people who
ever transgressed against us, but rather remember many against
whom we have transgressed. A multitude of people have been kind
and good to us and we are in debt to them. Saying with Paul,
"I am debtor," we mean that we have received something from
God, from Jesus Christ, from the church, from other people.

I OWE

To say that one is a debtor means also that one owes something.
It is interesting to note the different attitudes which people have
about their obligations. Some people deny that they have any. It
is indeed good if one can keep out of debt financially and owe nobody anything in dollars and cents. Paul admonishes to that end
in Romans 13:8: "Owe no one anything, except to love one another." This is good financial advice. But in life all together, who
can deny his indebtedness? How much we have received! It is
foolish to deny that we have any obligation. It is good to acknowledge it.

Some people ignore their debts. It is a mystery how a man can
do this, but we sometimes find that a person in great need reaches
out his hand and receives, then straightway forgets that he has
taken. There are people who, in order to get through school,
borrow large sums of money and immediately afterward appear
to forget about it completely. Oblivious, they go on their way, get-

ting many things for themselves and never thinking about paying back what they received when they themselves needed it badly.

Some people repudiate their debts. There is a legal process known as bankruptcy. This may be an instrument of mercy in time of great need. Perhaps no one can be sure that he will not sometime wish such mercy. Nevertheless, we read about partners, one of whom is worthless and flees into bankruptcy, while the other is left to manfully shoulder the whole load and, over a period of years, pay out the debt. Between the two characters we know the one which we admire the more. It is too bad to deny our honest indebtedness, or to ignore it, or to repudiate it.

Then there are people who pay back their debts. It is distinctive of Christianity, I think, that it makes people sensitive about this and eager to pay their debts. John Wesley tells about a man whom he misjudged. For a long time he thought of this person as miserly, niggardly, covetous. One day when he did not give a very large gift to a cause that was dear to Wesley, the latter exploded in indignation. The other, however, looked him straight in the eye and said, "I know a man who at the week's beginning goes to market and buys a few cents worth of parsnips and takes them home to boil in water, and all that week he has parsnips for his meat and the water for his drink, and meat and drink alike cost him a few cents a week." "Who is the man?" asked Wesley. "I am," replied the other. And Wesley wrote these words in his diary: "This he constantly did, although he then had an adequate income, in order that he might pay the debts he had contracted before he knew God. This was the man that I had thought to be covetous." When he came to know God, he wanted to pay his debts.

Sometimes we do not pay our debts back to the person from whom we have received, but we pay them only by passing on what we have received to somebody else. This too, I think, is a distinctive Christian insight, that debts can be paid in this way. Sometimes it is no longer possible to pay something back to the person from whom we got it, but we can still pay it back honestly and really by passing it on to somebody else. "I am debtor," says Paul, "both to Greeks and to barbarians." Many of these were people from whom he had never received anything. But he had received something wonderful from God and from Christ, and could pay it back by passing it on.

I WILL DO

To say that one is a debtor means furthermore that one will do something. Paul says, "I am debtor . . . so, as much as in me is, I am ready to preach the gospel to you also that are in Rome."[7] He will plan this trip to Rome. He will go beyond Rome, even to Spain,[8] to pay back his debt to God and Christ and the church and his fellow men. Working in the cause which Jesus inaugurated is a way of paying our debts.

The giving and the right using of money is also a way. At the very time that Paul was writing the letter to the Romans from which we have been quoting, he was engaged in taking up a collection among the churches of Macedonia and Greece to be carried to the poor saints at Jerusalem. Morton S. Enslin says that whenever Paul was called upon to raise money, he felt self-conscious about it.[9] Nevertheless he went ahead and did it. He was hard at work on that project at this very time. The next thing that he did was to journey to Jerusalem with the offering. His personal desire was to be off on his long-contemplated trip to Rome and Spain, but he went to Jerusalem instead in order to complete the project of the collection and deliver the money to the people for whose relief it was intended. As a matter of fact, the trip was made only at great peril to himself and he almost lost his life in the doing of it. He thought that the collection was something very significant in the program of Christianity. Using material resources aright is therefore a way of acknowledging indebtedness to God and Christ and the church and our fellow men.

When we say, "I am debtor," we mean, "I have received something." I certainly have. We mean, "I owe something." I certainly do. We mean, "I will do something." With divine help, I will.

The Centrality of Christ[1]

HAVING learned about Jesus Christ we have to go out into the world to live as his followers in the midst of the environment of our time. This environment is in many respects not so different from that in which the early followers of Jesus found themselves. When Paul, for example, came to Athens he was in a famous university center where there were distinguished teachers and students from far and near; and when he came to Corinth, he was in a commercial, cosmopolitan city where, coming from the wharves of the two nearby seaports of Cenchreae and Lechaeum, the traders and travelers of East and West met and mingled. As in the ancient world, so in the modern, education and business are major interests, and the surroundings and interests amidst which Paul found himself were probably similar in many regards to those in the world today.

So if we can note how Paul lived and worked then and there, we may find a clue as to how to live and work as Christians here and now. Paul has given us a statement on the subject in I Corinthians 2:2. Here he is thinking back to his time at Athens, and his going on over to Corinth. In a sentence he summarizes the program which he set for himself out of his experience. He says: "I decided to know nothing among you except Jesus Christ and him crucified."

THE STRATEGY OF PAUL

Paul concentrated on putting Christ at the center of life. The very wording of his statement suggests that he saw other possibilities and could have decided to do other things than he did. I suspect he was indeed tempted to take other approaches when he was in Athens and when he was in Corinth. When he was in Athens, I suspect it came to him that he might try to accommodate himself to the intellectual atmosphere of the place. It was, as we know, a place of rather idle skepticism and curiosity, but also of profound philosophical speculation. He might have made his major emphasis that of accommodation, checking at every point to see whether Christ agreed with Plato and Aristotle and the others before he ventured to say a word on his behalf.

When he went on to Corinth, I suspect he was tempted to syncretism, which was prevalent in that ancient world. This meant mixing together many deities and ideas into a composite religion. Above the city of Corinth was Acro-Corinth, the high hill with the temples of Aphrodite; across from the agora was the temple of Apollo. Why not come and speak about Christ simply as one more deity? One more or less did not matter too much to the ancient world. Paul could have presented his message much more easily on the basis of syncretism.

Wherever he went in the Roman Empire, he must have been tempted to compromise. From Augustus on, the Roman emperors took such titles as "Reverend" and "Son of God" and "God." At this time Nero, most blasphemous of them all, was on the throne. Ere long Domitian would reign, the ruler who was to persecute the Christians for their refusal to participate in emperor worship, which was regarded as a test of political loyalty and citizenship. The pressure for compromise must have been very great.

But if Paul had taken this general alternative, if his program and way had been that of accommodation and syncretism and compromise, then Christianity would have been rendered impotent. It would have been so fully adjusted to its environment that it would have had no power left to do anything about changing that environment.

When Paul, then, said that he decided to know nothing except Christ and him crucified, he must have been turning away from these possibilities. But was he turning to quite the opposite extreme?

Was he turning from accommodation to culture to repudiation of culture? At this point it may almost sound as if he were, but if we read his letters more fully we find that this was not the case. Paul wrote and spoke the Greek language. He looked with appreciation upon the Greek athletic contests and made references to them in his letters. This is no barbarian repudiating the culture in which he stands.

If Paul did not participate in the syncretism which prevailed, did he then spurn the religious quests of the time? Again no, for in his letters it is believed possible to detect references to the mystery religions, and allusions to the various ways in which men were then seeking God. If he did not compromise with the political organization, did he, at the opposite extreme, rebel against it? Yet again the answer is in the negative. In his letter addressed to the Romans, that is, to the Christians who lived under the very shadow of Nero's throne, Paul wrote some of the strongest words that have ever been written about the duty of a Christian citizen to the state in which he lives. It is well that Paul's program was not that of repudiation of culture, spurning of contemporary religious quests, and rebellion against the organization of society, for if it had been it would have rendered Christianity irrelevant to the needs of the time.

Thus Paul did neither what was on the one extreme nor on the other. What he did was to concentrate upon putting Christ at the center of culture, at the center of religion, and at the center of society. What John Wesley was to say many years later defines in other words what Paul undertook. John Wesley said, "I am a man sent of God to persuade men to put Christ at the center of their relationships."

THE RESULTS

What results follow when this is done? When Christ is put at the center, a great creative force is released. Look at those first three centuries of the Christian era. At that time the Greco-Roman culture and civilization appeared to be entering upon a period of stagnation. The great new energizing force which came in the first three centuries was the force of Christ. Under his inspiration and influence, the wonderful Greek language, which was being used for many a puerile and poor purpose, was lifted up to say such things as Paul said in I Corinthians 13: "If I speak in the tongues of men and of angels, but have not love, I am a noisy gong or a clanging cymbal." Art, under Christian influence, came to be used for the purpose of setting forth the everlasting meaning of life, showing human life, transient and brief as it is, in the setting of eternity. The message of that new Christian art still shines in the paintings on the walls of the catacombs beneath Rome. Architecture was employed for the construction of the early Christian basilicas, within the simple exteriors of which was the incredible richness of Biblical mosaics. Christianity entered culture as a creative force.

Look at another point in history. Take another three-century period—that from 1500 to 1800. At this time there was Reformation in both Protestantism and Roman Catholicism. This meant that the impact of Christ was felt afresh in the world. See what happened in two realms. Consider first the realm of thought. What great thinking was done! And at not a few points it is unmistakable that Christ had something to do with inspiring and influencing it. Among the prominent thinkers of the time, influenced by Christianity, were the following. Copernicus, the astronomer, was a man of the church. Giordano Bruno, the philosopher, although put to death by the Inquisition, had been a Dominican and always continued to believe in God as the unifying substance of the universe. Kepler, the great astronomer and mathematician, was trained originally for the ministry and departed from that course of life only reluctantly. Joseph Priestly, who discovered oxygen, was a clergyman. René Descartes, father of modern philosophy, had the background of the Roman Catholic church. John Locke, with whom the English Enlightenment began, was deeply impressed by the teachings of Jesus and was himself a product of the Puritan movement. Sir Isaac Newton, the mathematician, was even more interested in theology than in the realm of figures. Although remembered now primarily for his mathematics, he himself thought that his work in theology was the most important that he did. Immanuel Kant was brought up in a Pietist environment, and studied theology. These minds which were so influential in shaping the new channels of thought of that time came out of an earnest Christian environment, or developed a warm Christian faith for themselves. Mentioning these men, a cautious historian writes: "How far if at all the Christian faith of these men was responsible for the stimulus which made them intellectually creative we must not attempt to say. That some causal connection existed seems possible and even probable, but it would be impracticable to measure it accurately."[2]

Consider also the realm of music within the same period of three centuries. Music developed most remarkably, and the influence of Christ was evident in it. The oratorio derived its very name from musical services held in the oratory of St. Philip Neri in Rome. Palestrina did some of his most important work in writing music for the Mass. Bach was employed by the church and had his opportunity in it. Handel's oratorios centered on Biblical themes, and most of all proclaimed the Messiah. Hayden was trained in boyhood in a cathedral choir. Mozart was the son of a violinist in the service of the Archbishop of Salzburg. If music was so splendid in these centuries, it was in part because of the influence of Christ.[3] When Christ is made central in culture, there is introduced into it a creative force, the flowerings of which may appear in many directions.

Similarly, when Christ is put at the center of religious life, a surpassing fulfillment takes place. Professor Angus, who knows the religious quests of the ancient world intimately, says of Christianity's coming into that ancient world: "Christianity was the synthesis of and the authority for the truths proclaimed by all systems."[4] Synthesis is different from syncretism. In syncretism the result is an undifferentiated mass. In synthesis, the good things that are already there are caught up in a higher unity. That happens when Christ is made central in religion.

When Christ is made central in society, a tremendous transforming work is done. Speaking of the brief and apparently futile life of Christ, Kenneth S. Latourette says: "From that brief life and its apparent frustration has flowed a more powerful force for the triumphal waging of man's long battle than any other ever known by the human race. Through it, millions have had their inner conflicts resolved in progressive victory over their baser impulses. By it, millions have been sustained in the greatest tragedies of life and have come through radiant. Through it, hundreds of millions have been lifted from illiteracy and ignorance, and have been placed upon the road of growing intellectual freedom and of control over their physical environment. It has done more to allay the physical ills of disease and famine than any other impulse known to man. It has emancipated millions from chattel slavery and millions of others from thralldom to vice. It has protected tens of millions from exploitation by their fellows. It has been the most fruitful source of movements to lessen the horrors of war and to put the relations of men and nations on a basis of justice and peace."[5] These things do happen when Christ is put at the center of culture, of religion, and of society.

THE APPLICATION OF THE PRINCIPLE

In what parts of our daily lives may we ourselves seek to place Christ at the center? In the program of the church we may endeavor to make Christ central. It is our task and opportunity in the church to tell the story of the life of Jesus in the setting of the Bible; to do work of the kind which he did; and in all things to seek to have his spirit. If we do this first of all, then all the other ramified activities will fall into place around that center and all will be lifted up as by an incoming tide.

Practical affairs is another place where we may seek to make Christ central. The perplexities that confront us in doing it are many. It is easy to say that practical affairs must be handled in practical ways rather than in ways learned from Christ. Again and again, however, as practical men have pursued practical ways to do things on earth, they have turned out to be as strangely impractical as war itself is. Again and again Jesus has appeared as a realist when his way, tried bravely, has been found to work in practical affairs.

Finally, we may put Christ at the center as we build our philosophy of living. Each of us has some kind of philosophy. What shall we look at as we try to make a philosophy and live by it? Some people look at the atoms and, impressed by the law of indeterminacy, come out with a philosophy of chance and accident. Some look at the jungle and, seeing nature red in tooth and claw, emerge with a philosophy of strife. But Jesus Christ is as real a fact in this universe as the atoms or the jungle, and his life has a quality, a meaning, a significance far higher. If we look to him we, at last, may come to have a philosophy which is like that by which he himself lived so radiantly and triumphantly.

Here is how one young man did it. At the age of eighteen, as he himself later related, he was falling into sins which would have destroyed his character and was growing indifferent to religion. When he knelt down and prayed one night, it seemed as if God's presence was there, and it seemed as if he realized the nature of his own behavior more clearly than he had before. He wrestled with himself for a long time, and at last the voice of Christ seemed to speak to him and bring him peace. The next morning he went to church. When the minister pronounced the benediction at the close of the service, speaking of the grace of the Lord Jesus Christ and the peace of God, it seemed to him as if peace came back into his heart to abide. He says it stayed there all the rest of his life. It became practical for him to do work literally according to the teaching of Jesus in feeding the hungry. He went around the world and became a close associate of Mahatma Gandhi. His name was C. F. Andrews, and it came to be said that his initials—C.F.A.— stood for "Christ's Faithful Apostle." Mr. Andrews said of his experience: "Since then I may truthfully say that, in spite of very great suffering and terrible lapses and shortcomings, life has been happy and simple for me, and prayer a daily reality. In every part of the world, wherever I have gone, under all sorts of different conditions, while trying to serve mankind, I have had the joy of serving Christ. In this sense it has been more and more a reality for me to say, with all penitence, gratitude and love, 'For me, to live is Christ.' "[6]

CHAPTER TWENTY

Life's Ultimate Adventure

HOW SHALL a follower of Jesus face the ultimate question
in life, which is that of death? In the gospel according
to John we probably have the teaching of Jesus as appre-
hended in the profound reflection of a later disciple. There we find
the following statement as embodying the heart of what Jesus
taught on this question: "In my Father's house are many mansions."[1]

It will be necessary to look closely at the word "mansions." The
Greek word which occurs at this point may be translated "mansions," as in the Authorized and American Standard Versions; or
"rooms," as in the Revised Standard Version and the American
Translation of Edgar J. Goodspeed; or "abodes," as in the New
Translation by James Moffatt. It is no doubt usually assumed that
we have here the picture of a great house in which there are enough
rooms for all who come, where each may lie down in his own
place for eternal rest. The fundamental idea in the word is certainly that of a resting place or an abiding place, but it is not neces-
sarily implied that one is to rest and abide in a single place forevermore. Rather, the word may be used in the sense of a place to
stop for the night when traveling on a highway. In late Greek it was
definitely used with this connotation. The fourth gospel may have
been written at the beginning of the second century A.D., and at the
middle of the same century we find Pausanias using the identical
word in such a way that it is best translated "station." As a matter

of fact, our familiar "mansions" comes from the Vulgate translation, *mansiones,* and this word was employed by first and second century Roman writers like Pliny and Suetonius to refer to the stopping place at the end of a day's journey. It is regularly translated "night-quarters," "lodging place," or "inn." Both the Greek and the Latin suggest, therefore, that what is really meant in the saying in John is "stations," in the sense of overnight halting places upon a highway which leads further. "This appears to be the true meaning of the word here," says B. F. Westcott in his commentary on John 14:2, as he cites the usage: "resting-places, and especially the 'stations' on a great road where travellers found refreshment."[2]

THE ADVENTURE OF DEATH

Upon this interpretation, we may look forward to what lies beyond with a sense of adventure. Death itself is an adventure. Many times, of course, men come up to death through a period of suffering in which, in the mercy of God, their horizon is narrowed to only the most immediate of concerns. Or death may intervene with the swiftness of sudden accident. But upon a longer range view, death is actually an adventure. In relation to our own empirical knowledge, it is a going into the unknown. When the early geographers drew their maps they wrote across outlying areas of which they knew little or nothing, *terra incognita,* "unknown land." Death is *terra incognita* to human feet. It is "the undiscovered country," as Shakespeare said, "from whose bourn no traveler returns."

Dying is a going into the unknown, but it is a going to a land which we have reason to believe really exists. If to die were to enter into the unknown and there experience oblivion, as when the last spark dies out in a small pile of embers, or the flame of a candle is extinguished, that would hardly be adventure—it would be ultimate frustration. But if it is a going to a land in the actual existence of which we have reason to believe, then it is adventure.

In about A.D. 250 the geographer and astronomer Ptolemy drew a map of the world. The central part, which showed the Mediterranean region, was represented almost as accurately as by a modern geographer. More distant regions were less well known. The British Isles, the Scandinavian Islands (as he thought them to be), and India and Ceylon were indicated, but only very partially and with much distortion. Out beyond these were blank areas, where we now know continents to be—Australia and the Americas. On the map were also meridians of longitude, curving toward the north. Some of the ancient scientists had reached the conclusion that the earth is round. They had seen ships sail out from port and disappear over the horizon, the hull going down first and the masts dropping out of sight last. They had observed the shadow cast by the earth upon the moon in an eclipse, and noticed that it was curved. They had traveled from Greece to Egypt and had seen that certain constellations sank out of sight and others came into view. The hypothesis of the sphericity of the earth was reflected on Ptolemy's map in the curving lines of longitude. This map became known in Europe in the time of Columbus. When Columbus left Europe on his epochal voyage, he went into the unknown, yet he had reason to believe that he would come to another land.

Of course there were people who were skeptical. Hornell Hart has imagined a group of young positivists addressing Columbus like this: "Look here, Columbus. Nothing is real unless it's been measured by scientists. . . . This idea that the earth is round is a mere philosophical speculation. All that talk about India is just hearsay, and undoubtedly is based on mistaken interpretations of journeys to Persia. We positivists have every confidence that the well-measured parts of the world will ultimately prove to be the only ones that exist—or at any rate the only really important regions. These negations, if not quite beyond dispute, are yet so nearly certain that no system of thought which rejects them can hope to stand. We advise you, and all other wild-eyed and hare-brained navigators, to keep your little ships inside the Mediterranean, where the findings of geography are well established."[3]

This was written with conscious reminiscence of a famous paragraph of Bertrand Russell in which he speaks in the same way about any kind of philosophy that would suppose there is anything beyond the well-known limits of this scientifically described present mortal existence. Despite the skeptics, Columbus sailed with reason to believe there was something beyond. On the map of human thought and experience today the meridians curve toward the conclusion that there is a real world beyond this earthly existence to which we go when we die, in life's last great adventure. Here are two or three of the lines on the map which point to that conclusion.

There is the sense of the self within us, creative and time-transcending. We speak about personality with a twofold meaning. There is personality in the outward sense—the mask. This is the etymological meaning of the word. Then there is the other sense of personality, referring to the inward person, the inmost self. This is the central evaluative and creative self, which works to make the outward self what it ought to be. While the outward self changes across the years, the elements of the body being renewed and the patterns of behavior and manner of thought being altered, the inmost self continues to manifest that amazing persistence of personal identity to which we refer when we speak of the soul.

There is an intuition of the immortality of this inner self, the soul. This intuition is found in the life of earliest man. Neanderthal man, one hundred thousand years ago, and Cro-Magnon man, fifty thousand years ago, were burying their dead with tender care and placing in the grave objects and implements used and loved by the deceased during life, because they expected that they would live in the beyond, and need and use those same objects. The same intuition is represented by the poets. Tennyson writes:

> *Thou wilt not leave us in the dust:*
> *Thou madest man, he knows not why;*
> *He thinks he was not made to die;*
> *And thou hast made him: thou art just.*

An unknown soldier killed in World War I left these lines:

> *Why set this hunger for eternity*
> *To gnaw my heartstrings through,*
>   *if death ends all?*

Emerson said, "When God wants to carry a point with his children, he plants his argument in the instincts." Henri Bergson held that faith or intuition was a more native approach to truth than the approach of the intellect. Here in this widespread intuition of immortality is a fact that points to its reality.

Yet another line of thought that is curving toward the conclusion of immortality is this: unless there is immortality, our universe is neither rational nor good. The words of Professor George Herbert Palmer of Harvard University concerning the death of his talented wife, Alice Freeman Palmer, have become an almost classical statement on this point: "Though no regrets are proper for the manner of her death, who can contemplate the fact of it and not call the world irrational, if out of deference to a few particles of disordered matter it excludes so fair a spirit?"

Such are some of the lines on the map of thought which curve toward the stupendous conclusion that beyond that which is already known and experienced there is, out in the unknown, the real. That it is adventure to go thither has been held by many. Peter Pan, threatened with death as the water rose around the rock on which he was standing in the lagoon, cried: "To die will be an awfully big adventure." Charles Kingsley, lying on his deathbed, said: "God forgive me, but I look forward to it with an intense and reverent curiosity!" William Blake, the poet who wrote about building "Jerusalem in England's green and pleasant land" and about seeing "the World in a grain of sand, and a Heaven in a wild flower," said as he was dying that he was going to the country which he had wished to see all of his life. Don Blanding described the "Vagabond's Road":

> *Only for him who knows the ceaseless urge*
> *To . . . go ever on, carried by tide and trade-wind's pulsing surge,*
> *Lured by the bright mirage of far-off places,*
> *Forests and jungles and bleak frozen spaces. . . .*
> > *Knowing the spell*
> *That makes the Somewhere-else the Promised Land,*
> *Caring no whit if Sun of Surr or Samarkand*
> *Shall bleach his bones or curious creatures of the sea*
> *Play havoc with his flesh. . . .*

Ready to face that last dim misted trail
When eager eyes and pliant muscles fail,
Thinking of Death as just another place to go,
Another road to walk, another land to know.[4]

THE ADVENTURE OF IMMORTALITY

Dying will be an adventure because it will be going into the unknown, but to a land which we have reason to believe really exists. What, however, will be the conditions of continued life there? Without doubt we shall be weary and need to lie down to rest for a while. The idea of such repose is suggested in the text with which we are dealing, by the fact that the ancient "stations" were halting places for the night. But they were also the places from which the further journey began again each morning.

Therefore, there will be in immortality not only the repose which the tired soul needs but also the further progress for which the questing spirit longs. Instead of stagnation, as some popular expectation would have it, there will be the excitement of broader vistas and the adventure of traveling on a way which leads ever further. Commenting on the possible interpretation of "mansions" as "stations" in the text in John, Herbert Booth Smith says: "If this reading is correct, what an endless opportunity for adventurous and abundant living. What an encouragement to all the lives which never 'arrived' on earth, to all who were cut off before the song was sung and the picture painted and the vision realized."[5] On the same basis, Leslie D. Weatherhead writes: "Even death seems to mean just staying the night at an inn and then taking to the uphill road again, a road that ends beyond our vision in the high mountains of that perfection which is God's plan for every soul."[6]

It may be anticipated that there will be not only the possibility of progress in immortality but also the necessity of work. Halford E. Luccock, writing over the signature of Simeon Stylites in *The Christian Century,* has described a man who was always behind himself because he had so much work to do. He never got caught up. One night just before he went to sleep he thought to himself,

"If only once for twenty minutes in twenty years, I could catch up with myself!" Then he went to sleep and had this dream: He was in a beautiful room with a great mahogany desk, but on the desk there was not a single piece of paper. Looking out the window, he saw that the lawn was mowed and the car washed. There were no bills waiting to be paid, and no engagements written in his date book. "He had caught up with himself. Peace, perfect peace. Or was it? For around the edges of the peaceful vacuum there nibbled a little question: 'What do I do now?'" He saw a postman going by and called to him. He noticed that the postman had no letters or papers in his bag. There was nothing to deliver; he was just out for a walk. "Where am I?" asked the man. "This is hell," replied the postman cheerily.[7] Perhaps it was, for everything was caught up and there was nothing to do.

In immortality it may also be believed that there will be a finding of friends again. "Do they know us, love us, hope for our coming?" asks Lyman Abbott in *The Other Room*. "Shall we know them, love them, and may we hope for their fellowship? Surely. What is there left to be immortal in us if love and hope die? To exist without love and hope is not to live; to exist with hope always disappointed and love always denied would hardly be to live. What Scripture and philosophy alike promise to us is eternal life, not eternal sleep, and faith, hope, and love are the essentials of life."[8]

If there is progress, if there is work, and if there is love, then immortality will be adventure.

THE ADVENTURE NOW

It remains to say that the adventure can begin now. Jesus Christ has been raised from the dead. When we believe in him, we enter into his life. Those two great interpreters of Christ in the New Testament, John and Paul, agree in telling us this. John gives us the word of Christ: "I am the resurrection and the life; he who believes in me, though he die, yet shall he live, and whoever lives and believes in me shall never die."[9] Paul states: "We were buried therefore with him by baptism into death, so that as Christ was raised from the dead by the glory of the Father, we too might walk in newness of life."[10] So when we become Christians we enter upon the greatest adventure of all time, that of following Christ in an everlasting life. In that adventure we shall assuredly walk with him through some suffering and pain. But we shall also have the confidence that beyond every dark valley there will be the brightness of a new morning and, ultimately, of an eternal morning. The adventure is that of eternal life, of life now, and of life beyond life.

Notes

PREFACE

[1] *The Christian Century,* March 18, 1931. The quotations from *The Christian Century* are by permission of the editor.

CHAPTER 1. IN THE FULNESS OF TIME

[1] Romans 15:19. Unless otherwise noted, all New Testament quotations are from the Revised Standard Version (copyright 1946) and are by permission of the Division of Christian Education of the National Council of the Churches of Christ in the United States of America.

[2] I Corinthians 15:22.

[3] Galatians 4:4, American Standard Version. This and other quotations from the American Standard Version (copyright 1929) are by permission of the Division of Christian Education of the National Council of the Churches of Christ in the United States of America.

[4] Romans 5:6, American Standard Version and Revised Standard Version.

[5] *The Religious Situation* (1932), pp. 138 f. Quoted by permission of Henry Holt and Company, New York.

[6] *The Environment of Early Christianity* (1924), p. 1. Quoted by permission of Charles Scribner's Sons, New York.

[7] Revelation 18:12–13.

[8] Ecclesiastes 3:11. Unless otherwise noted, all Old Testament quotations are from the American Standard Version (copyright 1929), by permission of the Division of Christian Education of the National Council of the Churches of Christ in the United States of America. Where "Jehovah" occurs, "Lord" is substituted.

[9] Against Celsus, II, 30.

[10] Revelation 18:13.

[11] Galatians 3:28.

[12] Isaiah 9:2, 5–7, An American Translation. Quotations from this translation are by permission of The University of Chicago Press.

CHAPTER 2. THE HISTORIC JESUS

[1] Although entirely rewritten, material in this chapter was printed in *The Intercollegian,* September, 1948, and is used by permission. Likewise

material in chapters 2–5 was presented in Bible lectures at the 1948 International Convention of Disciples of Christ and, having been published in the book of convention addresses, is used with the permission of the International Convention of Disciples of Christ. Also, the writer has treated the subject of the present chapter in one chapter (XVI) of his *Like the Great Mountains* (St. Louis, Bethany Press, 1949).

[2] *The Creation of Christ,* tr. C. B. Bonner (1939), I, pp. viii, x. Quoted by permission of the publishers, Watts and Co., London.

[3] *The Witnesses to the Historicity of Jesus,* tr. Joseph McCabe, pp. 209 f. (Open Court Publishing Company, Chicago).

[4] *The Quest of the Historical Jesus,* tr. W. Montgomery (1910), pp. 5, 397. Quotations from this book are by permission of The Macmillan Company, New York.

[5] *The Beginnings of the Christian Church,* tr. B. L. Woolf (1937), pp. 54 f. By permission of Charles Scribner's Sons, New York.

[6] *History and the Gospel* (1938), p. 68. Quotations from this book are by permission of Charles Scribner's Sons, New York.

[7] *Jesus in the Light of History* (1942), p. 280. By permission of Charles Scribner's Sons, New York.

[8] Sanhedrin, 43a. Goldstein, *Jesus in the Jewish Tradition* (New York: The Macmillan Company, 1950), pp. 22, 31.

[9] *Did Christ Really Live?* (1938), pp. 27, 185. Quoted by permission of The Macmillan Company, New York. For an earlier book on the same subject see S. J. Case, *The Historicity of Jesus* (Chicago: The University of Chicago Press, 2nd ed., 1928).

CHAPTER 3. THE PROPHETIC JESUS

[1] *The Intellectual Adventure of Ancient Man* (1946), p. 224. Quoted by permission of The University of Chicago Press.

[2] *The Intention of Jesus* (1943), p. 1. Quotations from this book are by permission of The Westminster Press, Philadelphia.

[3] Mark 6:15.

[4] Mark 8:28.

[5] Matthew 21:11.

[6] Mark 6:4.

[7] Luke 13:33.

[8] Luke 4:16 ff.

[9] Zechariah 9:9.

[10] Matthew 21:7, An American Translation. This is a literal rendering of the Greek in this passage. The trouble the passage caused interpreters is attested by the corrections and variants which may be found in the various manuscripts at this point.

[11] Psalm 2:7.

[12] Isaiah 53:3.

[13] Ezekiel 2:1, An American Translation.

[14] *History and the Gospel,* p. 63.

[15] Mark 8:29.

[16] Matthew 11:27.

[17] Luke 22:37; Isaiah 53:12.

[18] *Jesus the Messiah* (1946), pp. 214 f. By permission of The Westminster Press, Philadelphia.

[19] *The Clue to History* (1939), p. 113. The quotations from this book are by permission of Harper and Brothers, New York.

[20] *Ibid.*, p. 96.

[21] Matthew 6:10.

[22] Isaiah 2:2, 4.

[23] Isaiah 11:6, 9.

[24] Isaiah 19:24–25.

[25] *The Predicament of Modern Man* (1944), p. 26. By permission of Harper and Brothers, New York.

[26] Isaiah 8:16, An American Translation.

[27] *The Clue to History*, p. 15.

CHAPTER 4. THE APOCALYPTIC CHRIST

[1] Elizabeth Hunter, "While Earth Remains," in *The Christian Century*, July 13, 1949.

[2] Ecclesiastes 3:20; 8:15, An American Translation.

[3] Daniel 7:27; 12:7.

[4] II Esdras 14:11, An American Translation.

[5] Revelation 11:3; 12:6.

[6] Mark 13:32.

[7] Matthew 23:37–38. Luke has the same words but places them earlier in the life of Jesus (13:34–35).

[8] Luke 21:34–35. The passage is in Luke alone. The other passages alluded to but not quoted in the text are Luke 12:35–38 and Luke 13:25, and are also to be found only in this gospel.

[9] *The Journal of Religion*, 28 (1948), p. 185. The quotations from this article are by permission of the editor of the *Journal*.

[10] Matthew 25:34.

[11] Luke 16:22. Only Luke records the story.

[12] *Le Royaume de Dieu et sa venue: Objet de l'espérance de Jésus et de S. Paul* (Paris: Félix Alcan, 1937), pp. 49 f., tr. Wilder in *The Journal of Religion*, 28 (1948), pp. 183 f.

[13] *Discerning the Signs of the Times* (1946), pp. ix-x. Quoted by permission of Charles Scribner's Sons, New York.

[14] Matthew 24:35; Mark 13:31; Luke 21:33.

[15] Matthew 26:29.

CHAPTER 5. THE PERSONAL CHRIST

[1] *The Quest of the Historical Jesus*, p. 4.

[2] *Ibid.*, p. 6.

[3] *Jesus and the Word*, tr. Louise P. Smith and Erminie Huntress (New York: Charles Scribner's Sons, 1934), p. 6.

[4] Mark 15:39.

[5] Matthew 28:19.

----

[6] Luke 24:32.

[7] *The Intention of Jesus,* p. 157.

[8] *The Quest of the Historical Jesus,* pp. 397, 401.

[9] *The Contemporary Christ* (1942), pp. 163 f. By permission of the publishers, Abingdon-Cokesbury Press, Nashville.

[10] Mark 8:28.

[11] Amos 1:3.

[12] Matthew 5:18, etc.

[13] *The Man Christ Jesus* (1941), p. 100. By permission of the publishers, Willett, Clark and Company, Chicago.

[14] *Pathways to the Reality of God* (1931), p. 143. By permission of The Macmillan Company, New York.

[15] *History and the Gospel,* p. 125.

[16] Luke 11:20.

[17] Luke 10:23.

[18] Luke 17:21.

[19] John 14:18.

[20] *The Works of Francis Thompson,* Poems: Volume II, p. 227. Quoted by permission of the publishers, Charles Scribner's Sons, New York.

CHAPTER 6. THE LIGHT OF THE WORLD

[1] Some of the ideas in this chapter were used in articles appearing in *Front Rank,* July 23 and 30, 1950, and these articles are drawn upon with the permission of the editor of that magazine.

[2] Romans 1:3.

[3] *The Historical Evidence for the Virgin Birth* (1920), p. 133. Quoted by permission of the Clarendon Press, Oxford.

[4] *Cold Morning Sky* (1937), pp. 52 f. By permission of The Macmillan Company, New York.

[5] Luke 1:76, 78, American Standard Version.

[6] *Anno Domini* (1940), p. 227. The quotations from this book are by permission of Harper and Brothers, New York.

[7] John 3:19.

[8] *Anno Domini,* p. 229.

[9] John 8:12; 9:5; cf. 12:46.

[10] Sukkah, 51a–52b.

[11] Luke 15:8.

[12] John 8:12.

CHAPTER 7. THREE CONCEPTIONS OF RELIGION

[1] James 2:19.

[2] Psalm 119:97, 54. Quotations from *The Bible: A New Translation* by James Moffatt, copyrighted 1922, 1935, and 1950 by Harper and Brothers, are used by permission.

[3] Galatians 5:6.

[4] *Heretics* (1905), pp. 158 f. By permission of John Lane The Bodley Head Ltd., London.

[5] Harry Emerson Fosdick, radio sermon, March 17, 1940. This and other quotations from his radio sermons are by permission of Dr. Fosdick.

[6] *Ibid.*

[7] *The Lost Radiance of the Christian Religion* (1924), pp. 9 f. By permission of George H. Doran Company, New York.

[8] The Epistle to Diognetus, 5–6.

CHAPTER 8. THE INGREDIENTS OF HAPPINESS

[1] Ecclesiastes 1:18, An American Translation.

[2] Quoted by Harry Emerson Fosdick in a radio sermon, February 18, 1940.

[3] "The Simple Things," from *Collected Verse* by Edgar A. Guest; copyright 1934, by the Reilly and Lee Co., Chicago.

[4] In *The Christian Century,* September 14, 1949.

CHAPTER 9. IF THINE EYE BE SINGLE

[1] Mark 5:9.

[2] Mark 3:24 f.; James 1:8.

[3] Hazen G. Werner, *And We Are Whole Again* (Nashville: Abingdon-Cokesbury Press, 1945), p. 135.

[4] *Shadows on the Rock* (1931), p. 149. Quoted by permission of Alfred A. Knopf, New York.

[5] Matthew 13:44.

CHAPTER 10. WHEN HE CAME TO HIMSELF

[1] *On Being a Real Person* (1943), p. 122. Quoted by permission of Harper and Brothers, New York.

CHAPTER 11. THE RETICENCE OF CHRIST

[1] Luke 12:13 f.

[2] John 8:5, 7, 10 f.

[3] Mark 13:4, 32.

[4] Mark 15:2.

[5] Luke 16:31.

CHAPTER 12. WHEN THE LAMP SMOLDERS

[1] Isaiah 42:3 quoted in Matthew 12:20, Authorized Version.

[2] Mark 9:24.

[3] Luke 8:24, American Standard Version.

[4] Luke 23:42 f.

[5] *Reader's Digest,* February, 1949. By permission of the editors.

CHAPTER 13. THE NIGHT COMETH

[1] Genesis 8:22.

[2] Luke 13:32.

[3] *Prayer* (1942), p. 37. Quoted by permission of Abingdon-Cokesbury Press, Nashville.

[4] *Mr. Jones Meet the Master* (1949, 1950), p. 15. By permission of Fleming H. Revell Co., New York.

[5] Mark 2:20.

[6] Billy Rose in the *Reader's Digest,* September, 1949. Quoted by permission of Mr. Rose.

[7] *1000 Quotable Poems, An Anthology of Modern Verse,* compiled by Thomas C. Clark and Esther A. Gillespie (Chicago: Willett, Clark and Company, 1937), II, pp. 157 f. By permission of Dr. Clark.

CHAPTER 14. HE TOOK IT UPON HIMSELF

[1] Luke 2:49.

[2] Luke 3:23.

[3] Mark 10:45.

[4] John 18:2.

[5] John 10:18.

[6] Isaiah 53:4–6.

[7] Luke 12:48.

[8] Romans 15:1, A New Translation by James Moffatt.

[9] *He Took It upon Himself* (rev. ed. 1930), pp. 37 f. By permission of the Pilgrim Press, Boston.

CHAPTER 15. CHRIST AND JERUSALEM

[1] Mark 13:1.

[2] Luke 19:41–44.

[3] *New York Times,* January 10, 1951.

[4] Otto Dibelius in *The Christian Century,* January 31, 1951.

[5] Luke, 19:45.

[6] John 2:15.

[7] Mark 3:5; 10:14.

[8] Galatians 6:7.

[9] *Days of Our Years* was published by Hillman-Curl, Inc., New York, in 1939.

[10] From *Poems, Essays and Letters* by Joyce Kilmer. Copyright 1914, 1917, 1918 by Doubleday & Company, Inc. By permission.

CHAPTER 16. LORD, IS IT I?

[1] Matthew 26:22, American Standard Version.

[2] II Samuel 12:7, 13.

[3] Matthew 7:3.
[4] *Preaching Values in New Translations of the New Testament* (New York: Abingdon Press, 1928), p. 26.
[5] Matthew 7:1.
[6] *When the Lamp Flickers* (1948), pp. 159 f. The quotations from this book are by permission of Abingdon-Cokesbury Press, Nashville.
[7] Jeremiah 17:9.
[8] Matthew 26:31; Zechariah 13:7.
[9] Matthew 26:33 f.
[10] Matthew 26:26, 28.
[11] Acts 20:7.
[12] This book was published by Doubleday, Doran and Company, New York, in 1929.

CHAPTER 17. FATHER, FORGIVE THEM

[1] Mark 15:26.
[2] I Corinthians 2:8.
[3] Mark 2:16.
[4] Mark 2:24.
[5] Mark 3:22.
[6] *Good Friday and Other Poems* (1916), pp. 51 f., 54. By permission of The Macmillan Company, New York.
[7] Matthew 18:21 f.
[8] Matthew 5:24.
[9] Matthew 6:9, 12.
[10] *Secrets of Effective Living* (1927), pp. 134 f. The quotations from this book are by permission of The Macmillan Company, New York.
[11] *The Life and Words of Christ* (rev. ed. 1925), II, p. 531. By permission of D. Appleton and Company, New York.
[12] I John 2:1.
[13] *Secrets of Effective Living*, pp. 135 f.

CHAPTER 18. I AM DEBTOR

[1] Romans 1:14, American Standard Version.
[2] Romans 1:1–3.
[3] Psalm 103:2 f.
[4] Romans 1:4 f.
[5] Romans 1:8.
[6] Romans 16:3 f., 7.
[7] Romans 1:15.
[8] Romans 15:24.
[9] *Christian Beginnings* (New York: Harper and Brothers, 1938), p. 257.

CHAPTER 19. THE CENTRALITY OF CHRIST

[1] Some of the material in this chapter was printed in *Front Rank*, April 30, 1950, and is used by permission of the editor.

[2] Kenneth S. Latourette, *Anno Domini*, pp. 139 f.

[3] For these and other examples see also Latourette, *op. cit.*, pp. 143 f.

[4] *The Environment of Early Christianity*, p. 225.

[5] *Advance through Storm* (1945), pp. 503 f. By permission of Harper and Brothers, New York.

[6] *Federal Council Bulletin*, November, 1931.

CHAPTER 20. LIFE'S ULTIMATE ADVENTURE

[1] John 14:2, American Standard Version.

[2] *The Gospel according to St. John, The Greek Text with Introduction and Notes* (London: John Murray, 1908), II, p. 167.

[3] *Skeptic's Quest* (1938), p. 101. By permission of The Macmillan Company, New York.

[4] *Vagabond's House* (1937), Preface. By permission of Dodd, Mead and Company, New York.

[5] *The Pulpit*, April, 1950. By permission of the editor.

[6] *When the Lamp Flickers*, p. 202.

[7] *The Christian Century*, February 14, 1951.

[8] *The Other Room* (1904), pp. 91 f. By permission of The Macmillan Company, New York.

[9] John 11:25.

[10] Romans 6:4.